Sexual Consent

Other Books of Related Interest

Opposing Viewpoints Series
Human Trafficking
LGBTQIA+ Rights
The #MeToo Movement

At Issue Series
Male Privilege
Mob Rule or the Wisdom of the Crowd?
Sexual Consent

Current Controversies Series
America's Mental Health Crisis
Microaggressions, Safe Spaces, and Trigger Warnings
Political Correctness

> "Congress shall make no law ... abridging the freedom of speech, or of the press."
>
> *First Amendment to the U.S. Constitution*

The basic foundation of our democracy is the First Amendment guarantee of freedom of expression. The Opposing Viewpoints series is dedicated to the concept of this basic freedom and the idea that it is more important to practice it than to enshrine it.

Sexual Consent

Lisa Idzikowski, Book Editor

Published in 2025 by Greenhaven Publishing, LLC
2544 Clinton Street,
Buffalo, NY 14224

Copyright © 2025 by Greenhaven Publishing, LLC

First Edition

All rights reserved. No part of this book may be reproduced in any form without permission in writing from the publisher, except by a reviewer.

Articles in Greenhaven Publishing anthologies are often edited for length to meet page requirements. In addition, original titles of these works are changed to clearly present the main thesis and to explicitly indicate the author's opinion. Every effort is made to ensure that Greenhaven Publishing accurately reflects the original intent of the authors. Every effort has been made to trace the owners of the copyrighted material.

Cover image: Srijaroen/Shutterstock.com

CataloginginPublication Data

Names: Idzikowski, Lisa, editor.
Title: Sexual consent / edited by Lisa Idzikowski.
Description: First edition. | Buffalo, NY : Greenhaven Publishing, 2025. | Series: Opposing viewpoints | Includes bibliographical references and index.
Identifiers: ISBN 9781534509870 (pbk.) | ISBN 9781534509887 (library bound)
Subjects: LCSH: Sexual consent. | Sexual ethics. | Sex and law.
Classification: LCC HQ32.S498 2025 | DDC 176'.4--dc23

Manufactured in the United States of America

Website: http://greenhavenpublishing.com

Contents

The Importance of Opposing Viewpoints	11
Introduction	14

Chapter 1: How Are Sexual Consent and Sexual Assault Defined?

Chapter Preface	18
1. Sexual Consent Is More than No Means No *Jacqueline Hendriks*	19
2. With Affirmative Consent, Yes Means Yes *Rachael Burgin*	25
3. Drugs and Alcohol Complicate the Issue of Sexual Consent *Alex Aldridge*	31
4. How Common Are Rape and Sexual Assault in the United States? *Sarah L. Coo*	35
5. What Exactly Is Sexual Consent on College Campuses? *Tovia Smith*	42
Periodical and Internet Sources Bibliography	49

Chapter 2: How Does Culture Affect Sexual Consent?

Chapter Preface	51
1. India Continues to Blame Women in Sexual Crimes *Erin Watson-Lynn*	53
2. Girls and Women Are Exploited by the Media *Swagata Sen*	58
3. A Culture of Patriarchy Leads to Rape Culture *Robert Jensen*	64

4. The #MeToo Movement Brings Sexual Assault
   Out in the Open   73
   Jessalynn Keller
5. Women Are Not the Only Victims of Sexual
   Assault and Abuse   79
   Joan M. Cook and Amy Ellis
6. How Religion Can Prevent Sexual Consent   84
   Vicki Lowik and Annabel Taylor

Periodical and Internet Sources Bibliography   89

Chapter 3: Is Sex Work Consensual?

Chapter Preface   92
1. Sex Work Is Often Considered Sex Slavery   93
   Carly Daniel-Hughes
2. Sex Work Is a Choice, Not Exploitation   101
   Angela Jones
3. Sex Work Abolitionists Deny Sex Workers Agency   107
   Victoria Bateman
4. There Are Ways to End Violence Against
   Sex Workers   123
   Jayne Swift
5. Does It Make Sense to Decriminalize Sex Work?   129
   Naomi Grimley

Periodical and Internet Sources Bibliography   134

Chapter 4: How Will the Topic of Sexual Consent Continue to Evolve?

Chapter Preface   137
1. Has the #MeToo Movement Gone Off Track?   138
   Michel Martin
2. Young People Are Using the Internet to
   Promote Sexual Consent and Education   146
   Chloe Krystyna Garcia

3. Catholic Church Sex Abuse Must Be Punished and Stopped *BBC*	**153**
4. Sexual Consent Alone Is Not Enough *Nicole M. Jeffrey*	**160**
Periodical and Internet Sources Bibliography	**165**
For Further Discussion	**167**
Organizations to Contact	**169**
Bibliography of Books	**173**
Index	**174**

The Importance of Opposing Viewpoints

Perhaps every generation experiences a period in time in which the populace seems especially polarized, starkly divided on the important issues of the day and gravitating toward the far ends of the political spectrum and away from a consensus-facilitating middle ground. The world that today's students are growing up in and that they will soon enter into as active and engaged citizens is deeply fragmented in just this way. Issues relating to terrorism, immigration, women's rights, minority rights, race relations, health care, taxation, wealth and poverty, the environment, policing, military intervention, the proper role of government—in some ways, perennial issues that are freshly and uniquely urgent and vital with each new generation—are currently roiling the world.

If we are to foster a knowledgeable, responsible, active, and engaged citizenry among today's youth, we must provide them with the intellectual, interpretive, and critical-thinking tools and experience necessary to make sense of the world around them and of the all-important debates and arguments that inform it. After all, the outcome of these debates will in large measure determine the future course, prospects, and outcomes of the world and its peoples, particularly its youth. If they are to become successful members of society and productive and informed citizens, students need to learn how to evaluate the strengths and weaknesses of someone else's arguments, how to sift fact from opinion and fallacy, and how to test the relative merits and validity of their own opinions against the known facts and the best possible available information. The landmark series Opposing Viewpoints has been providing students with just such critical-thinking skills and exposure to the debates surrounding society's most urgent contemporary issues for many years, and it continues to serve this essential role with undiminished commitment, care, and rigor.

The key to the series's success in achieving its goal of sharpening students' critical-thinking and analytic skills resides in its title—

Opposing Viewpoints. In every intriguing, compelling, and engaging volume of this series, readers are presented with the widest possible spectrum of distinct viewpoints, expert opinions, and informed argumentation and commentary, supplied by some of today's leading academics, thinkers, analysts, politicians, policy makers, economists, activists, change agents, and advocates. Every opinion and argument anthologized here is presented objectively and accorded respect. There is no editorializing in any introductory text or in the arrangement and order of the pieces. No piece is included as a "straw man," an easy ideological target for cheap point-scoring. As wide and inclusive a range of viewpoints as possible is offered, with no privileging of one particular political ideology or cultural perspective over another. It is left to each individual reader to evaluate the relative merits of each argument—as he or she sees it, and with the use of ever-growing critical-thinking skills—and grapple with his or her own assumptions, beliefs, and perspectives to determine how convincing or successful any given argument is and how the reader's own stance on the issue may be modified or altered in response to it.

This process is facilitated and supported by volume, chapter, and selection introductions that provide readers with the essential context they need to begin engaging with the spotlighted issues, with the debates surrounding them, and with their own perhaps shifting or nascent opinions on them. In addition, guided reading and discussion questions encourage readers to determine the authors' point of view and purpose, interrogate and analyze the various arguments and their rhetoric and structure, evaluate the arguments' strengths and weaknesses, test their claims against available facts and evidence, judge the validity of the reasoning, and bring into clearer, sharper focus the reader's own beliefs and conclusions and how they may differ from or align with those in the collection or those of their classmates.

Research has shown that reading comprehension skills improve dramatically when students are provided with compelling, intriguing, and relevant "discussable" texts. The subject matter of these collections could not be more compelling, intriguing, or urgently relevant to today's students and the world they are poised to inherit. The anthologized articles and the reading and discussion questions that are included with them also provide the basis for stimulating, lively, and passionate classroom debates. Students who are compelled to anticipate objections to their own argument and identify the flaws in those of an opponent read more carefully, think more critically, and steep themselves in relevant context, facts, and information more thoroughly. In short, using discussable text of the kind provided by every single volume in the Opposing Viewpoints series encourages close reading, facilitates reading comprehension, fosters research, strengthens critical thinking, and greatly enlivens and energizes classroom discussion and participation. The entire learning process is deepened, extended, and strengthened.

For all of these reasons, Opposing Viewpoints continues to be exactly the right resource at exactly the right time—when we most need to provide readers with the critical-thinking tools and skills that will not only serve them well in school but also in their careers and their daily lives as decision-making family members, community members, and citizens. This series encourages respectful engagement with and analysis of opposing viewpoints and fosters a resulting increase in the strength and rigor of one's own opinions and stances. As such, it helps make readers "future ready," and that readiness will pay rich dividends for the readers themselves, for the citizenry, for our society, and for the world at large.

Introduction

> "Consent is an agreement that is willfully given without any external pressure or factors. In order for someone to consent to sexual activity participants must continuously communicate—before, during, and after sexual activity."
>
> —*The American Sexual Health Association*

Sexual consent is not a new issue. American lawmakers once had the age of consent as young as 10 or 12 years old for girls, this being based on English laws dating back to the 1500s. By the late 1800s in the United States, an organization comprised of women called the Woman's Christian Temperance Union (WCTU) rallied against this. Through much action and petition the WCTU managed to get the age of consent raised to 14 or 16 in some states. They vowed to keep working as they wanted the age to be increased to 18.

What exactly is sexual consent? According to Planned Parenthood, sexual consent "is an agreement to participate in a sexual activity. Without consent, sexual activity is sexual assault or rape." It's important to note that Planned Parenthood also contends that a person needs to know if the other person wants to engage in sexual activity too. And both engaged parties must agree to the sexual activity every single time in order for it to be considered consensual—consenting to an activity once doesn't guarantee consent in perpetuity. Scholars at Harvard University argue that "consent must be present during the initiation and throughout the

Introduction

duration of sexual activity to distinguish it from sexual assault." Furthermore, according to the White House, sexual assault is a common problem across the United States and the globe. President Joe Biden insists that "freedom from sexual assault is a basic human right."

Not surprisingly, the media, popular culture, religion, and patriarchy all have a hand in questions around consent. Another factor is geography. Certain regions around the world struggle with issues relating to male dominance, rape culture, and lax laws and prosecution of sex crimes. Some religious groups are known to practice a form of control over women by dictating that women and girls should be subservient to their husbands and fathers. Men raised in these traditions see it as their duty to be the head of the family and control the women and children in their lives. Research also has shown that this can lead to inappropriate, nonconsensual sexual behavior.

Another segment of society makes the issue of sexual consent even muddier. Sex work adds a level of complexity to the question of sexual consent. In 2016, over half of adults in the United States said that it was immoral to work as a sex worker. But over half of men thought it should be legalized, and about the same number of women thought it should remain illegal. However, many experts today insist that sex work is work, and that many individuals involved in the sex trade do so to support themselves and their families. They assert that people who engage in sex work should be offered legal protections that protect them from sexual assault, rape, and other forms of violence, but in order for sex work to be regulated it would have to be legalized. Opponents contend that sex work is by nature nonconsensual because the people who engage in it are coerced by the offer of money.

Amidst all this complexity, is there a way to bridge the gap between moral concerns surrounding sex and the need to ensure that sexual consent is clearly defined and considered a requirement in our society? Many experts in the education field say that early and continuous teaching about consent is a way to the future.

Beginning in grade school and at home, consent must be modeled and taught. Other researchers agree that sex education must be mandatory for young people. They believe that it is a disservice to limit sex education to abstinence only programs, and that this ultimately prevents young people from gaining necessary knowledge about sexual consent. Statistics demonstrate that abstinence only programs foster the kind of thinking that makes sexual consent almost impossible to give when it is necessary. Finally, there are examples in the world where countries have experimented with different strategies relating to sex work. It is worth considering both the negative and positive outcomes of these programs.

This timely debate surrounding the issue of sexual consent is explored in *Opposing Viewpoints: Sexual Consent*. Readers will obtain valuable insight and understanding into this divisive and ongoing contemporary issue.

CHAPTER 1

How Are Sexual Consent and Sexual Assault Defined?

Chapter Preface

Sexual consent is a complex issue. To some it is characterized by the phrase "no means no." Others think of it in terms of "yes means yes." It is about respecting yourself and your right to control what happens to your body and respecting other people's right to bodily autonomy as well. A big part of ensuring this happens is through good communication—actively seeking affirmative, enthusiastic answers before proceeding with any physical activity.

How many people are taught about consent, and where are they taught about consent? Some educators argue that this should be taught in schools starting at an early age before individuals end up on college campuses. At universities there is often a big mix of young people with new freedoms, parties, and alcohol. The question then becomes, can sexual consent be given under the influence of alcohol, or any other mind and body altering substances? Schools around the United States are grappling with these thorny issues. What causes sexual activity to cross the line and become sexual assault, or even rape? How commonly do these occur?

Another facet of discussions about sexual consent is the role of language in the issue. If sexual consent is not taught in schools across the country, does everyone speak the same language when it comes to this delicate subject? Does consent mean the same thing to everyone? Could that complicate matters when two people find themselves interacting in private matters such as sex?

The viewpoints in this chapter shine a light on these ideas that surround the topic of sexual consent and how concepts related to sexual consent and assault are defined.

VIEWPOINT 1

> "We should be careful not to oversimplify the issue of consent. Sexual negotiation can be a difficult or awkward process for anyone—regardless of their age—to navigate."

Sexual Consent Is More than No Means No

Jacqueline Hendriks

In the following viewpoint Jacqueline Hendriks reports on the curriculum being used in Australian schools to teach about consent. Hendriks outlines the things that students should learn but notes that this varies widely between schools. Hendriks also notes that the issue of consent does not just apply to sexual activity, but to many other aspects of life, making it an essential lesson for all young people. Since questions of consent do not have to specifically apply to sexual activity, it is possible to also teach younger students about it in an age-appropriate way. Jacqueline Hendriks is a research fellow and lecturer at Curtain University in Australia.

As you read, consider the following questions:

1. How is consent defined in this viewpoint?

"Not as simple as 'no means no': what young people need to know about consent", by Jacqueline Hendriks, The Conversation, February 22, 2021. https://theconversation.com/not-as-simple-as-no-means-no-what-young-people-need-to-know-about-consent-155736. Licensed under CC BY-ND 4.0 International.

2. As reported by the author, how many Australian students have been in an unwanted sexual experience?
3. As stated by Hendriks, who is not able to give consent?

A recent petition circulated by Sydney school girl Chanel Contos called for schools to provide better education on consent, and to do so much earlier.

In the petition, which since Thursday has been signed by more than 5,000 people, Contos writes that her school

> … provided me with life-changing education on consent for the first time in year 10. However, it happened too late and came with the tough realization that amongst my friends, almost half of us had already been raped or sexually assaulted by boys from neighboring schools.

So, what core information do young people need to know about consent? And is the Australian curriculum set up to teach it?

What's in the Curriculum?

This is not the first time young people have criticized their school programs. Year 12 student Tamsin Griffiths recently called for an overhaul to school sex education after speaking to secondary students throughout Victoria. She advocated for a program that better reflects contemporary issues.

Australia's health and physical education curriculum does instruct schools to teach students about establishing and maintaining respectful relationships. The resources provided state all students from year 3 to year 10 should learn about matters including:

- standing up for themselves
- establishing and managing changing relationships (offline and online)
- strategies for dealing with relationships when there is an imbalance of power (including seeking help or leaving the relationship)

- managing the physical, social and emotional changes that occur during puberty
- practices that support reproductive and sexual health (contraception, negotiating consent, and prevention of sexually transmitted infections and blood-borne viruses)
- celebrating and respecting difference and diversity in individuals and communities.
- Despite national guidance, there is wide variability in how schools interpret the curriculum, what topics they choose to address and how much detail they provide. This is further compounded by a lack of teacher training.

A study of students in South Australia and Victoria, along with repeated nationwide surveys of secondary students, have shown young people do consider school to be a trustworthy source of sex education. But most don't believe the lessons have prepared them adequately for relationships and intimacy.

They want lessons that take into account diverse genders and sexualities, focus less on biology, and provide more detail about relationships, pleasure and consent.

The national curriculum also stops mandating these lessons after year 10 and many year 11 and 12 timetables are focused on university entrance exams or vocational learning opportunities. This means senior students have limited opportunity to receive formal sex education at a time when they really need it.

So, What Should Young People Know About Consent?

The term "consent" is often associated with sex, but it's much broader than that. It relates to permission and how to show respect for ourselves and for other people. Consent should therefore be addressed in an age-appropriate way across all years of schooling.

The most important point about consent is that everyone should be comfortable with what they're engaging in. If you are uncomfortable at any point, you have the right to stop. On the other side, if you see someone you are interacting with being uncomfortable, you need to check in with them to ensure they are enthusiastic about the activity, whatever it may be.

In the early years, students should be taught how to affirm and respect personal boundaries, using non-sexual examples like whether to share their toys or give hugs. It is also important they learn about public and private body parts and the importance of using correct terminology.

In later years, lessons should consider more intimate or sexual scenarios. This also includes consent and how it applies to the digital space.

Older students need to learn sexual activity is something to be done *with* someone, not *to* someone. Consent is a critical part of this process and it must be freely given, informed and mutual.

Consent isn't about doing whatever we want until we hear the word "no." Ideally we want all our sexual encounters to involve an enthusiastic "yes."

But if your partner struggles to say the word "yes" enthusiastically, it is important to pay attention to body language and non-verbal cues. You should feel confident your partner is enjoying the activity as much as you are, and if you are ever unsure, stop and ask them.

Often this means checking in regularly with your partner.

Young people also need to know just because you have agreed to do something in the past, this does not mean you have to agree to do it again. You also have the right to change you mind at any time—even partway through an activity.

It's Not as Simple as 'No Means No'

The most recent Australian survey of secondary school students highlighted that more than one-quarter (28.4%) of sexually active students reported an unwanted sexual experience. Their most common reasons for this unwanted sex was due to pressure from a partner, being intoxicated or feeling frightened.

How Are Sexual Consent and Sexual Assault Defined?

We should be careful not to oversimplify the issue of consent. Sexual negotiation can be a difficult or awkward process for anyone—regardless of their age—to navigate.

Some academics have called for moving beyond binary notions of "yes means yes" and "no means no" to consider the grey area in the middle.

While criminal acts such as rape are perhaps easily understood by young people, teaching materials need to consider a broad spectrum of scenarios to highlight examples of violence or coercion. For example, someone having an expectation of sex because you've flirted, and making you feel guilty for leading them on.

When it comes to sexual activity, we should be clear that:

- although the law defines "sex" as an activity that involves penetration, other sexual activities may be considered indecent assault
- a degree of equality needs to exist between sexual partners and it is coercive to use a position of power or methods such as manipulation, trickery or bribery to obtain sex
- a person who is incapacitated due to drugs or alcohol is not able to give consent
- wearing certain clothes, flirting or kissing is not necessarily an invitation for other things.
- We should also challenge gender stereotypes about who should initiate intimacy and who may wish to take things fast or slow. Healthy relationships involve a ongoing and collaborative conversation between both sexual partners about what they want.

Consent Is Sexy

A partner who actively asks for permission and respects your boundaries is showing they respect you and care about your feelings. It also leads to an infinitely more pleasurable sexual experience when both partners are really enjoying what they are doing.

It is important that lessons for older students focus on the positive aspects of romantic and sexual relationships.

They should encourage young people to consider what sorts of relationships they want for themselves and provide them with the skills, such as communication and empathy, to help ensure positive experiences.

VIEWPOINT 2

> "Affirmative consent... shifts from a 'no means no' standard to 'yes means yes,' in that an individual seeking to have sex with another person must obtain clear, expressed consent from them before (and while) engaging in a sexual act."

With Affirmative Consent, Yes Means Yes

Rachael Burgin

In the following viewpoint Rachael Burgin reports on laws introduced in Australia to promote affirmative sexual consent. Burgin outlines how this legislation will affect teaching in schools, and in the end, help prevent sexual violence. The new legislation would raise the standards for proving belief in consent for individuals accused of sexual assault, creating a greater burden of proof for the accused in sexual assault cases. They would also have the effect of shifting attitudes away from the notion that women and other sexual assault victims act or dress in a way that invites sexual activity. Dr. Rachael Burgin is a senior lecturer in criminology and criminal justice at Swinburne Law School in Melbourne, Australia.

"NSW adopts affirmative consent in sexual assault laws. What does this mean?", by Rachael Burgin, The Conversation, May 21, 2021. https://theconversation.com/nsw-adopts-affirmative-consent-in-sexual-assault-laws-what-does-this-mean-161497 Licensed under CC BY-ND 4.0 International.

Sexual Consent

As you read, consider the following questions:

1. According to the viewpoint, what is a simple way to obtain consent?
2. What is affirmative consent, as explained by the author?
3. According to Burgin, what will prevent sexual violence?

New South Wales Attorney-General Mark Speakman has announced a suite of reforms to consent law, following a two-and-a-half year review by the Law Reform Commission.

The review was prompted by survivor-advocate Saxon Mullins, who endured two trials and two appeals, only to end up with no legal resolution to her rape case. Since then, Mullins has advocated for affirmative consent.

However, the final report from the commission, released in November last year, failed to recommend this standard. Despite this, Speakman has stood alongside Mullins with the promise of a bill that goes beyond the recommendations of the commission— and will make affirmative consent the law in NSW.

What Is Affirmative Consent?

Affirmative consent means that consent is *actively* sought and *actively* communicated. This approach shifts from a "no means no" standard to "yes means yes," in that an individual seeking to have sex with another person must obtain clear, expressed consent from them before (and while) engaging in a sexual act.

In other words, submission without active, participatory agreement is not sufficient to claim that consent was given. In practice, this could be something as simple as asking someone if they want to have sex.

This type of consent standard shifts the emphasis from the actions of the victim-survivor to those of the accused. This is important, since we know that the same rape myths and gendered stereotypes that permeate society can be brought sharply to bear in sexual assault trials.

Despite this, and international shifts towards affirmative consent, governments across Australia have been hesitant to legislate it, and Law Reform Commissions are apparently loathe to recommend it.

In addition to the NSW Commission, the Queensland Law Reform Commission earlier this year also failed to recommend affirmative consent, opting instead to recommend no substantive change to consent law. That report was heavily criticized as relying largely on research that had not been peer-reviewed, and ignoring recent Australian academic research.

The Changes in New South Wales

The bill announced today changes that course. Speakman has presented reforms that go beyond the Law Reform Commission's recommendations and, if enacted, would legislate affirmative consent in NSW.

This is because the bill requires that a person who is seeking to raise the defense of "reasonable belief in consent" must demonstrate what actions they took or what words they spoke to ensure they had consent. A failure to do or say something (that is, to "take steps") to ascertain consent means that any belief in consent will not be reasonable.

This is affirmative consent in action—and it takes its lead from the law in Tasmania, which has operated without controversy for nearly two decades.

It is also where other jurisdictions fall down. Victoria, for example, is often heralded as a leader in affirmative consent. However, my research analyzing rape trial transcripts from the County Court of Victoria shows that defense counsel continue to rely on narratives of victim resistance or "implied consent," that construct women's ordinary, everyday behavior as indicating consent.

This is, as I have argued, because Victoria does not require an accused person to show they did anything to ensure their

> ## Teens and Children Are Unable to Legally Sexually Consent
>
> ### The Law Indicates Who Can Consent to Sex and Who Cannot
>
> The law recognizes that children are developmentally not able to make decisions about some things, including when to engage in sexual behaviors. Laws vary by state, but a common age of consent is 16. Engaging in sexual behaviors with someone under the age of consent is illegal and will be treated as criminal sexual conduct.
>
> ### A Child's Permission Does Not Equal Legal Consent
>
> Even if a child or underage teen gives permission or acts willingly, this never implies consent. A child is never accountable. A child's permission or even request to play a sexual touching or watching game never excuses the adult or teen from taking full responsibility for the interaction.

potential sexual partner was consenting. If a person did take steps to ascertain consent, they are able to raise this in their defense.

However, the reasonableness of a belief in consent, in Victoria, can be built exclusively on the accused person's perception of the victim-survivor's conduct—whether she was drinking alcohol, wearing certain types of clothing, dancing near him or not offering enough "resistance" to his sexual advances.

The NSW government has sought to respond to these problems that continue to plague Victorian courts by making these consent steps mandatory. This means the NSW provision will act as a protection to victim-survivors in their pursuit of justice, and will protect from prosecution accused people who, even in their mistake, acted reasonably.

It is always the adult's responsibility to set boundaries with children and underage teens. Sometimes people justify their sexual activity with children by saying the child "wanted" to or the child touched them first. They may misread a child's affection as sexual. They may tell themselves "Age is just a number" or "They look and acts older so it's okay." If someone you know is unclear about boundaries with children, remind them of their responsibility to set boundaries and the potentially high consequences to them if they don't.

Learn the Laws in Your State

If your teen is in a romantic relationship with a younger peer, it is important to talk with them about the laws about consent. Be sure they understand the importance of the age differences between two sexually active teens and at what age they can legally consent to sexual contact—and when the laws says they can't. Learn the laws in your state and talk with your child about the potentially serious consequences of not following the law. You can find this information online or learn more through the local office of your Attorney General.

"Why Permission from a Child or Underage Teen Doesn't Count," STOP IT NOW!.

What Does This Mean?

The ethos that a person who wants to have sex should make sure their potential partner also wants to should underpin both our responses to and prevention of sexual violence.

This approach can set the framework for how we teach young people—or "re-teach" older generations—about consent, relationships and sexuality. In the context of a rape trial, the hope is that affirmative consent will go some way to ensuring that attitudes which blame women for their victimization, and excuse sexual violence, do not play a role in the outcome.

This does not, as some may claim over the next few months as we see this bill progressing through parliament, reverse the onus of proof. People accused of sexual assault will continue to be afforded their right to the presumption of innocence.

However, this bill does place an evidential burden on an accused person who seeks to raise a defense of reasonable belief in consent to show they took steps. The onus remains on the prosecution to disprove this once the defense has discharged its evidential burden.

A Win for Survivors

The NSW reforms are a huge win for survivors, particularly Saxon Mullins, who catapulted consent onto the public and political agenda.

But it is not the end of the story. The law, while holding potential to set community expectations, is—and should be—the avenue of last resort. Attention must also be paid to preventing sexual violence before it occurs.

VIEWPOINT 3

> "*The gender of the people having sex, their sexuality, the nature of their relationship and how they became intoxicated – whether willingly or unwillingly – all shape the judgements that we make about intoxicated consent.*"

Drugs and Alcohol Complicate the Issue of Sexual Consent

Alex Aldridge

In the following viewpoint Alex Aldridge explores the controversial argument that women cannot truly have informed consent when it comes to sexual encounters because of the power differential between the sexes caused by patriarchy. Because women are not on equal footing with men, they are not really "free" to make decisions about sex. Aldridge explores the ways in which power dynamics, mainstream attitudes toward sexuality, and substances impact consent. And finally, Aldridge reports that sexual consent is not viewed the same across all countries. Alex Aldridge was a PhD candidate at the Royal Holloway University of London at the time this viewpoint was published.

"Drugs and alcohol complicate sexual consent, but context can make things clearer", by Alex Aldridge, The Conversation, November 21, 2018. https://theconversation.com/drugs-and-alcohol-complicate-sexual-consent-but-context-can-make-things-clearer-106207 Licensed under CC BY-ND 4.0 International.

Sexual Consent

As you read, consider the following questions:

1. As explained by the viewpoint, can women ever have informed consent?
2. What is chemsex, according to Aldridge? What are the potential dangers it poses?
3. As stated by the author, how does sexual consent differ in other countries?

Sexual consent is an important, complex and often awkward topic to talk about. And when people have been consuming alcohol or other drugs, it makes negotiating sexual consent even more complicated. Indeed, drawing the line between consensual sex and assault when a complainant is heavily intoxicated is a particularly difficult area of law.

What is clear though, is that context matters. The gender of the people having sex, their sexuality, the nature of their relationship and how they became intoxicated—whether willingly or unwillingly—all shape the judgements that we make about intoxicated consent.

The importance of context was brought to the forefront in the late 1970s and early 1980s, when the so-called "feminist sex wars" divided Western academics who were interested in gender equality. The debates were dominated by arguments over pornography and sex work, but the issue of sexual consent—and what it means for women living in a patriarchal society—was always present.

Context and Consent

Influential legal scholar Catharine MacKinnon drew attention to society being organized in such a way that men hold the power; women's consent and sexuality is, to some extent, conditioned and controlled by these power structures. MacKinnon's contemporary, Andrea Dworkin, took this argument further. She claimed that women's subordination underpins male sexual desire.

So, to give and receive consent meaningfully, there needs to be an awareness of the power dynamics at play, and the impact they have on the relationships among people. This raises questions about just how meaningful women's sexual consent can be under patriarchy. When women are not on an equal footing with men, are they really "free" to make choices about sex with those men?

Others have highlighted the role that sexuality plays in shaping mainstream views about sexual consent. For example, anthropologist Gayle Rubin has argued that historically, sexual consent has been a privilege afforded only to those who engage in socially accepted (or even socially encouraged) sexual behavior—that is, heterosexual, monogamous, procreative sex. In the UK, as recently as 1997, the age of consent was higher for same-sex sexual activity than it was for heterosexual sex. So, even if individuals were freely choosing such sexual activity, their consent was not legally recognized.

Assumptions around gender and sexuality also affect the way people think about intoxicated sexual consent today. For example, consider the public response to the so-called chemsex phenomenon: chemsex refers to the intentional use of drugs—often methamphetamine, GHB and mephedrone—to enhance and prolong sexual encounters between men who have sex with men.

Chemsex has largely been portrayed as a public health crisis, with an emphasis on the potential for the transmission of HIV. Yet little attention is paid to the sexual violence and exploitation men might well experience in chemsex settings. By contrast, when chemsex is discussed in relation to heterosexual people, the issue of sexual consent moves to the forefront.

A Worldwide Survey

It's useful to reflect on how categories such as gender and sexuality—and indeed race, ability and social class—might affect the way intoxication and sexual consent are talked about and understood. But while these categories are important, they are not enough to explain why certain intoxicated sexual experiences are perceived by those involved as consensual, and others not.

Based on an earlier project, for which Aldridge spoke with a diverse group of people who had had sex on drugs, it seems that in order to understand the complexity of intoxicated consent, it's necessary to probe further into the specific contextual elements of sex on drugs. That might include the settings in which this activity takes place (sex club, house party, music festival), the type of drug being consumed (MDMA, cannabis, alcohol) and the nature of relationship between those having sex (one-night stand, long-term relationship, group sex).

Intoxicated consent can be negotiated successfully, but understanding how these other contextual factors affect sexual relationships is vital to addressing situations where it's not. At present, only a fraction of sexual assault incidents are reported and even fewer result in convictions.

In 2013, the Global Drug Survey began to explore people's experiences of intoxicated sexual consent. Out of 22,000 people, 20% reported having had been taken advantage of while intoxicated, while 5% said that this had happened in the last year. What's more, 14% reported that they had been given drugs or alcohol by someone who intended to take advantage of them.

This year, the Global Drugs Survey is delving deeper. Researchers will be collecting contextual information from people who have been taken advantage of while intoxicated, including where they were, who they were with, their relationship with the person or people who took advantage of them and the type of drug they were using.

Cultural norms and tolerance for such behaviors vary between countries. Because the 2019 survey is translated into 22 languages, researchers will be able to compare outcomes across regions. The aim of this survey is to give a voice to those unable to speak out. The findings will be used to shape interventions that minimize harm and maximize support for people who have experienced sexual assault, while ensuring that perpetrators are correctly identified, and held responsible.

VIEWPOINT 4

> *"The fear of sexual harassment and assault—terms that encompass everything from unwanted touching, grabbing and kissing to rape and attempted rape—is all too common among women in the U.S. and around the world."*

How Common Are Rape and Sexual Assault in the United States?

Sarah L. Coo

In the following viewpoint Sarah L. Coo analyzes the issue of sexual harassment and rape in the United States by zeroing in on statistics taken from college campuses and other venues. Coo argues that many women feel a constant threat that sexual violence may happen to them at some point in their lives. Surprisingly, Coo uses stats from the 1950s and 1960s to argue that attitudes have not gotten better on this issue over the intervening decades. Sarah L. Coo is a professor and associate dean at Georgia State University. She is a nationally recognized expert on violence against women.

"How common are sexual harassment and rape in the United States?", by Sarah L. Coo, The Conversation, November 21, 2018. https://theconversation.com/how-common-are-sexual-harassment-and-rape-in-the-united-states-67358. Licensed under CC BY-ND 4.0 International.

Sexual Consent

As you read, consider the following questions:

1. According to the viewpoint, what is a fear that many women live with?
2. How many college women experience rape, as stated by the author?
3. What has changed over the years about men's attitudes centered around sexual violence, according to Coo?

"I have moved in the world as a woman and a man. I never realized the absence of fear, and the feeling of invulnerability until I lived as a man."

These were activist Max Beck's parting words to my Psychology of Women course in 2005. Beck, born intersexed, lived in a body manipulated by medical intervention to be a girl and then a woman. In adulthood, having learned that when he was born, his sex was unclear, he chose to live the last years of his life as a married and devoted father.

Max spoke about an invisible, ever-present sense of vulnerability that for many women is palpable. The fear of sexual harassment and assault—terms that encompass everything from unwanted touching, grabbing and kissing to rape and attempted rape—is all too common among women in the U.S. and around the world. A student at the University of Alabama poignantly wrote, "Something that's always in the back of my mind: One day, one of these victims could be me."

But is this sense of vulnerability grounded in data? Are women really at high risk?

This week Fox News anchor Megyn Kelly has talked about her allegations of sexually predatory behavior by her former boss Roger Ailes. This comes in the wake of similar allegations against Bill Cosby and President-elect Donald Trump.

Each time these stories hit the headlines, the public is appalled and shocked. Yet, years of social science data underscore the pervasive scope of sexual violation in women's lives. I have been conducting research on violence against women for a quarter-century. The sad truth is that despite public outrage, sexual harassment and assault continue to be as widespread a problem today as they were 25 years ago.

The Experience on Campus

The practical, methodological and ethical challenges to conducting scientific research on sexual harassment and assault are many. Harassment and assault usually occur in private, the experiences are highly stigmatized and victims feel such shame that they rarely make a report to authorities. Yet, researchers began to attempt to understand women's experiences of assault nearly 60 years ago.

In 1957, sociologist Eugene Kanin found that 62 percent of a sample of college freshmen women had experienced "offensive and displeasing attempts at necking, petting above... [and] below the waist, sexual intercourse, and/or a more violent attempt at sexual intercourse accompanied by menacing threats or coercive infliction of physical pain." Kanin's language may sound strange to young people today, but the questions he asked clearly describe experiences that today we would label nonconsensual sexual contact to attempted rape.

The results of Kanin's study, however, remained hidden in scholarly journals.

It was only 30 years later, in 1987, that nationally representative data on the nature and scope of sexual aggression on college campuses were disseminated widely through the popular book "I Never Called It Rape" by Robin Warshaw.

Warshaw's book translated psychologist Mary Koss and colleagues' groundbreaking scholarly study of date and acquaintance rape for the general public. This study is the source for the famous "one in four" statistic: that about a quarter of college women report experiences equivalent to rape, that few label their experiences as rape and even fewer report their experiences to authorities.

Two methodologically similar studies conducted between 1995 and 1997 confirmed the findings of the 1987 study.

And when a broader range of nonconsensual sexual acts are considered (for example, groping or unwanted kissing), many more women on campus are affected.

In Koss' study, 28 percent of women reported having experienced such episodes when they were as young as 14. In a separate study 10 years later, nearly 10 percent of college women reported unwanted and attempted unwanted sexual contact within a single academic year.

Recently, researchers at the University of Oregon responding to the White House Task Force's call for information were surprised to find that nearly 60 percent of women graduate students reported experiences of sexual harassment.

Women at Risk Everywhere

Other groups of women face similar or higher risk.

Data from the National Crime Victimization Study, analyzed by criminologists Callie Rennison and Lynn Addington, show that economically disadvantaged women are at slightly higher risk of being raped than college women. In 2010 the Centers for Disease Control and Prevention estimated that 20 percent of American women overall have experienced rape. Women who identify as bisexual report far more rape, as do multiracial and Alaskan/American Indian women. Others, such as lesbian and Latina women, report far less.

Similar nationally representative data on women's experiences of sexual harassment do not exist, but an analysis of different studies of women in academia, government, the private sector and the military (86,000 women in all) documented that 58 percent said they had experienced at least one instance of sexually harassing behavior.

Whether perpetrators target specific groups of women, whether some groups of women underreport assault more than others or whether other factors are responsible for some women being at higher risk than others continue to be unanswered questions.

How Many Men Perpetrate Harassment or Assault?

So what do the data say about the number of men who perpetrate sexual harassment and assault?

In his 1969 study on men, Kanin concluded that—based on his study at one academic institution—about 25 percent of men reported committing at least one "sexually aggressive episode" since entering college. Kanin noted that these episodes would "usually not be sufficient violent to be thought of as rape attempts" although "these aggressions involved forceful attempts at removing clothing and forceful attempts to maneuver the female into a physically advantageous position for sexual access." These episodes clearly meet the FBI definition of attempted rape.

Nearly 20 years after Kanin's study, in the first nationally representative study of its kind, 8 percent of men reported having raped or attempted rape. When the scope was broadened to all forms of sexual assault, the percent of men who reported nonsexual contact increased to 25.

Since 1987, however, no national studies on how often rape and other forms of sexual assault or harassment are perpetrated have been federally funded or conducted privately.

One source of available data on sexual harassment is the military.

The Navy is making some progress to understand sexual harassment—67 percent of just over 1,000 U.S. Navy men in their first year of service reported that they had sexual harassed women. This included giving unwanted attention to women and making "crude sexual remarks either publicly or privately," as well as "threatening women with some sort of retaliation for not being sexually cooperative."

The relative dearth of data on harassment and assault perpetration is perplexing, given the widespread calls to prevent this behavior. To know whether prevention strategies work, we must have accurate and current knowledge of how often such behavior occurs.

The fact is that despite decades of raising awareness and providing education, rape and other forms of sexual assault and harassment remain pervasive threats in women's and men's lives. They are akin to normal and expected aspects of the feminine and masculine experience.

High-profile incidents, such as Donald Trump's blatant description of his behavior and Gretchen Carlson's and Megyn Kelly's allegations of Roger Ailes' sexual harassment of network staff, stimulate public discussion.

These debates come at a terrible cost to the women who come forward publicly. Their motivations are questioned. Their experiences diminished. But if they continue, they have the chance to see social norms change. And the dialogue is present on a scale never before seen.

Those who insist that the number of women who are victimized is overstated, or that the experiences are far less traumatic than portrayed, or that women make false accusations, will always exist.

But what has changed is that an increasing number of men are opposing victim-blaming, calling out reprehensible behavior and seeking justice for victims, as Vice President Joe Biden did after Brock Turner was sentenced to six months for sexually assaulting an unconscious woman. During this election season, the discussion included new voices, with many expressing outrage because they were husbands, fathers, brothers of women. Prominent commentators, such as *The New York Times*' Frank Bruni, went further, opposing outrage based on men's relationships with women and arguing that all should speak out about assaults on all women.

This election season kept sexual harassment and assault in the national consciousness. Recent advances in preventive interventions focus not on potential perpetrators but on promoting community norms that counter attitudes and behaviors that support harassment and assault.

This national discussion has moved us beyond choreographed campaigns where sports figures and other celebrities proclaim opposition to rape and sexual assault. We are seeing the opposition in real time through responses to Trump's hot mic moment, language during debates and threats of harm through social media.

Now that Trump is president-elect, his actions, past and present, will keep the issue top of mind.

Could this added focus mean the day is near when the ever-present and unnamed threat of harassment and assault leaves women's lives?

VIEWPOINT 5

> "As the federal government presses colleges to improve the way they handle cases of sexual assault, schools are turning their focus to defining 'consent'—how to distinguish between activity that's consensual and activity that's not."

What Exactly Is Sexual Consent on College Campuses?

Tovia Smith

In the following viewpoint Tovia Smith analyzes the tough topic of sexual consent and how it is defined on college campuses around the country. Smith presents examples from a number of campuses showing what consent should sound like and/or look like. Despite changing attitudes and increased attention to creating a culture of consent at colleges throughout the country, Smith shows how complicated sexual consent on university campuses still can be. Tovia Smith is an award-winning national correspondent for National Public Radio (NPR) based in Boston.

As you read, consider the following questions:

1. What is an example of behavior that would indicate that consent has been given, as stated by Smith?

©2014 National Public Radio, Inc. NPR news report "A Campus Dilemma: Sure, 'No' Means 'No,' But Exactly What Means 'Yes'?" by Tovia Smith was originally published on npr.org on June 13, 2014, and is used with the permission of NPR. Any unauthorized duplication is strictly prohibited.

2. Is verbal consent a good option, according to the viewpoint?
3. Should schools be the ones defining sexual consent, according to this viewpoint?

As the federal government presses colleges to improve the way they handle cases of sexual assault, schools are turning their focus to defining "consent"—how to distinguish between activity that's consensual and activity that's not.

On one level, it's obvious. As the old line goes, "You know it when you see it." But less obvious is how to spell it out for the student handbook. There are about as many different definitions of consent as there are colleges.

"If consent were easy to put into words, we'd have a sentence, and we wouldn't have a page and a half of definition," says Mary Spellman, dean of students for Claremont McKenna College, which recently rewrote its definition.

As with most colleges, the bulk of Claremont McKenna's definition covers what's *not* consent. That's the easier part. For example, any OK from someone who's drunk or drugged or coerced can never count as consent. And consent to have sex last weekend or even an hour ago can't imply consent now.

But the definition also tries to get at those grayer areas, like when a student may be ambivalent or when something ends up happening that a student never intended.

Claremont McKenna's definition says permission has to be "clear, knowing and voluntary," but it also has to be "active, not passive." So a student who's silent, for example—or not resisting—is by definition not consenting.

"I don't think [the definition] is perfect," Spellman says. "I think it's come a long way, but I think we will find over time that it will evolve."

Only 'Yes' Means 'Yes'

The trend now, and what the White House recommended in its recent guidance to colleges, is toward what's called "affirmative

The Difference Between Assent and Consent

Assent vs Consent–Don't Lie to Get Laid!

Permission is a form of *assent*. But *consent* has a different meaning in the eyes of the law. And that distinction makes tricking someone, or depriving them of consent in any other way, a crime.

By law, *consent,* not *assent,* must be present in sexual relations, as stated clearly in the *ItsOnUs Pledge*, supported by President Obama; *"Non-consensual sex is sexual assault."* Assenting, not consenting to sex, simply doesn't cut it!

What's the Difference Between Assent and Consent?

The University of Alaska, Fairbanks, points out (in adherence with federal Nuremberg Code) that such a difference exists in its description of the legal requirements when conducting ethical research on minors:

> Work with children or adults not capable of giving consent requires the consent of the parent or legal guardian and the assent of the subject.

From this description, we can easily see that *assent* and *consent* don't carry the same weight. Even though the explanation is given to facilitate a purpose not related to sexual conduct, it's clear that there is a legal distinction between *assent* and *consent*. And this

consent." In other words, instead of the old "no means no," the idea now is that only "yes means yes."

But even that still leaves room for interpretation—or misinterpretation—since "yes" can be expressed nonverbally.

"Is the person actively participating?" says Spellman. "Are they touching me when I am touching them? Are they encouraging me when I'm doing various different things? Those would all be signs that the person is an active participant in whatever is going on."

How Are Sexual Consent and Sexual Assault Defined?

distinction is at the heart of why any sexual conduct, even those containing assent, but not consent, is criminal.

Assent Simply Means "Agreement on the Face of It." Consent Means "Freely Given, Knowledgeable and Informed Agreement."

Just because you nod your head and provide permission to something, does not mean you were fully informed, and being fully informed of the action AND the actor is absolutely essential to qualify as consent. The use of force or duress, such as violence or fear that your career will cease, constitute sex without consent. Agreement when concerned about harm is acquiescence, not consent.

In all types of sexual assault, the offender knows they have deprived you of the ability or freedom to make your informed choice. They deliberately clouded your judgment. When you are under the influence of alcohol or drugs, or when you are unconscious, even though you may assent, the offender knows you are incapable of consent.

Assenting to an action means agreeing, but when that agreement was induced by force duress or deception, the person is *unknowing*, therefore, not *consenting*. Having sex with you, without your fully informed agreement, robs you of your self determination over your reproductive organs. All sex in which the victim is deprived of consent, or tricked to think their assent is consent, should be outlawed in every state and around the world!

"Assent vs. Consent—They're Not One and the Same!," by Joyce M. Short, Consent Awareness Network.

To try to make it a little more clear, some schools amend their definitions with a series of explicit scenarios that read like sexual consent word problems. Yale offers two pages of them.

In one example, "Tyler and Jordan are both drinking heavily.... Tyler becomes extremely drunk. Jordan offers to take Tyler home ... [and] ... initiates sexual activity.... Tyler looks confused and tries to go to sleep. Jordan has sex with Tyler."

Yale prints the answer in italics: *"There was no consent to have sex. . . . The penalty would be expulsion."*

But other examples are trickier. One describes two friends, Morgan and Kai, who are engaging in sexual activity in Kai's room. Morgan "looks up at Kai questioningly" before escalating the activity and "Kai nods in agreement" so Morgan proceeds. But when Kai reciprocates, "Morgan lies still for a few minutes, then moves away, saying it is late and they should sleep."

On that one, Yale says that Kai wrongly assumed that it was OK to reciprocate *"but took no steps to obtain unambiguous agreement. The . . . penalty would likely be a reprimand."*

"When you see these scenarios, you understand that this is something that is complicated," says Rory Gerberg, a student at Harvard's Kennedy School of Government who helped advise the White House on its recent guidance for schools. She says these kinds of hypotheticals are critical to showing students what "loud and clear" consent actually looks like.

Carefully crafted legal definitions are one thing, Gerberg says, "but knowing what that actually means in their life on a Friday or Saturday night is different."

A clear definition is critical not only to educate students, but also for the adjudication process. Just ask Djuna Perkins, a former prosecutor who now consults with colleges as an investigator of complaints and is the one left trying to sort through the murky question of whether a student's actions amounted to a nonverbal "yes."

"The fact of the matter is that consent is very tricky, and you're getting into minutiae of what happened in a particular event," she says. "It will sometimes boil down to details like who turned who around, or [whether] she lifted up her body so [another student] could pull down her pants.

"There have been plenty of cases that I've done when the accused student says, 'What do you mean? [The accuser] was moaning with pleasure. He was raising his body, clutching my back, exhibiting all signs that sounded like this was a pleasurable event.'"

Perkins says schools are being asked to define consent more narrowly than even most state criminal laws do. And the stakes couldn't be higher; those who get it wrong risk not only lawsuits and bad press, but also the loss of federal funding. The federal government is already investigating at least 55 schools for complaints that they're too soft on sexual assault.

"Some [schools] feel like they want to throw up their hands," Perkins says. "I know of colleges who are trying to revise their policies literally every summer. In this climate, I don't think there's a single school out there that really, truly feels like it's under control."

Antioch's Approach

Some schools have tried to avoid the ambiguity by mandating that students get explicit verbal permission before making any sexual advance. (The only way around the rule is if students have a prior verbal agreement to use a pre-arranged hand signal.)

"It's on them to say, 'Can I do this?' And the person has to respond verbally, 'Yes.' And if they don't, it's considered nonconsent, and that's a violation of our policy," says Louise Smith, dean of community life at Antioch College.

Smith says consent by Antioch's definition has to be clear and enthusiastic. "I guess so" wouldn't cut it. Also, the Antioch definition says consent must be continually renewed each time things escalate to "each new level of sexual activity."

The policy actually goes back to the early 1990s, when it was seen as so extreme it was mocked on *Saturday Night Live*. "Yeah, we're not laughing now," says Smith. She says Antioch feels vindicated because the rest of the country is finally coming around.

Smith says students are also beginning to realize that getting verbal consent doesn't have to be awkward or a mood killer.

"Yeah, it can be hot, like, 'Do you like it when I bite your neck?' " says Rebecca Nagle, co-founder of a group called Force: Upsetting the Culture of Rape, which runs campus workshops and a website using the slogan "Consent Is Sexy."

"We can be making out, and I can be like, 'So, how do you feel about teeth?' " Nagle says. "And if I have a certain look in my eye, that's really flirty. And then, I can be like, 'Do you like it like this?' And that exchange is incredibly hot," she says.

Nagle says students are starting to understand that it's better to deal with asking—even if it does feel forced—than with a morning-after accusation that the sex was nonconsensual. But as others see it, colleges are overstepping by trying to script what students should say in the dark of their dorm rooms and by imposing an unfair standard.

"Students will have their lives maybe seriously damaged by administrators who are essentially creating standards by the seat of their pants," says Anne Neal, president of the American Council of Trustees and Alumni. She worries that the stricter standards come with no due process for the accused, who face the burden of proving they did have enthusiastic and continual consent.

Neal says allegations of sexual assault should be handled by the criminal justice system, not schools. "To allow bureaucrats on our college campuses arbitrarily to determine what is consent and what is not, when even the law has difficulty, certainly underscores the absurdity of this system," she says.

But pressure on colleges is only increasing, both from the government and from their own students.

Murylo Batista, a junior at Dartmouth College, has been pressing his school to narrow its definition of consent. He says he's shocked by how many students still don't get it and are unsure the morning after if they crossed the line.

"That freaks me out!" he says. "How do you not know if you raped someone or not? That is pretty scary to me."

Batista says colleges are not the only ones who have to do more to help young people understand the meaning of consent. In order for students to really get it, he says, the lesson needs to start long before students even get to college.

Periodical and Internet Sources Bibliography

The following articles have been selected to supplement the diverse views presented in this chapter.

Cydney Adams, "Can Drunk Sex Ever Be Consensual?" CBS, April 26, 2019. https://www.cbsnews.com/news/can-drunk-sex-ever-be-consensual-cbsn-originals/.

Brandon Barnett, "What Is the Age of Consent in the United States," BHW Law Firm, August 13, 2016. https://www.bhwlawfirm.com/legal-age-consent-united-states-map/.

Katharine Drabiak, "Human Rights Report and Age of Consent for Sex Laws," Harvard Law, May 4, 2023. https://blog.petrieflom.law.harvard.edu/2023/05/04/human-rights-report-and-age-of-consent-for-sex-laws/.

Jennifer A. Drobac, "Age-of-Consent Laws Don't Reflect Teenage Psychology. Here's How to Fix Them," Vox, November 20, 2017. https://www.vox.com/the-big-idea/2017/11/20/16677180/age-consent-teenage-psychology-law-roy-moore.

Elizabeth Gulino, "Can You Consent to Sex If You're Drunk? The Answer Seems Clear, But Not Everyone Agrees," Refinery29, July 6, 2021. https://www.refinery29.com/en-us/sex-consent-alcohol.

Rachael Pace, "How to Understand Sexual Consent in Healthy Relationships," marriage.com, March 16, 2023. https://www.marriage.com/advice/physical-intimacy/sexual-consent/.

Neil Shouse, "Is It Illegal for Two Minors to Have Sex? A Lawyer Explains," Shouse California Law Group, March 14, 2024. https://www.shouselaw.com/ca/blog/is-it-illegal-for-2-minors-to-have-sex/.

Grace J. Wojdak, "Catholics Should Care about Sex and Consent," *America*, October 12, 2023. https://www.americamagazine.org/faith/2023/10/12/consent-sex-marriage-246249.

Olivia Wynkoop, "How Conversations about Consent Cast Out Queer Relationships," Golden Gate Xpress, April 9, 2021. https://goldengatexpress.org/97116/city/how-conversations-about-consent-cast-out-queer-relationships/.

Chapter 2

How Does Culture Affect Sexual Consent?

Chapter Preface

Without a doubt, culture affects the issue of sexual consent. One could question what influence media plays in sexual consent issues. Historically, movies, print media, social media, and other media forms have portrayed women as objectified sexual beings in some contexts, and this is an ongoing issue. However, some movies, TV shows, books, and social media influencers are now working to draw attention to the issue of sexual consent and increase awareness. Along with media, common cultural institutions also affect how people understand sexual consent issues. This is seen, for example, in how various religious institutions preach that women should behave and submit to their husbands in a marriage.

Attitudes towards this issue vary in different cultures around the world as well. For instance, in recent years countries like India have been grappling with this social issue. Patriarchy is an ancient belief that continues into modern times throughout much of the world. This belief is understood as men having dominance over women and children in the family and society. When women are expected to submit to men, it makes it difficult to leave room for sexual consent. Not surprisingly, there are misunderstandings surrounding this contentious issue, such as whether only women and girls suffer from the negative effects of sexual assault or intimate partner abuse. Depictions in the media have led to this stereotype, but more recent studies indicate that sexual assault and abuse sadly is also widespread among men and boys and within the LGBTQIA+ community.

The viewpoints in this chapter explore the function of media, religious beliefs, cultural practices and values, and cultural campaigns such as the #MeToo movement with respect to sexual consent. Some viewpoints in this chapter blame media for displaying women in submissive roles, which they assert has a detrimental impact on sexual consent. Other viewpoints expose how entrenched beliefs such as patriarchy, cultural norms, and religious convictions can promote abuse and mistreatment. Still others explore how media and cultural institutions can play a positive role in promoting a culture of consent.

VIEWPOINT 1

> "There is an enduring history of victim-blaming culture in India, from political elite through to convicted criminals."

India Continues to Blame Women in Sexual Crimes

Erin Watson-Lynn

In the following viewpoint Erin Watson-Lynn reports on the cultural custom of blaming victims of sexual crimes in India. Watson-Lynn maintains that India has an enduring history of victim-blaming which has had a detrimental impact on the safety of women. She explains some of the examples of sexual assaults that are taking place in India and some of the attempts to stop this cultural problem. She also points out that although the viewpoint focuses on this issue in India, it is certainly not a problem that is specific to that country alone. Erin Watson-Lynn is a foreign affairs advisor working for universities, governments, and think tanks. She has published numerous academic papers and opinion pieces leading publications.

As you read, consider the following questions:

1. What are two causes of sexual crimes in India mentioned in this viewpoint?

"India: Still blaming victims " by Erin Watson-Lynn, Lowy Institute, June 30, 2019. Reprinted with permission.

Sexual Consent

2. As reported in this viewpoint, do boys blame girls in sexual assault crimes in India?
3. What is the "panic button" that is being tried out in India, as reported by the author?

Last year, I wrote in the *Interpreter* about Modi's panic button policy approach to increasing concerns about women's safety in India.

Fast forward seven months and on New Year's Eve, in the south Indian city of Bengaluru (formerly Bangalore), women were harassed, groped, and assaulted en masse. News about the mass molestation rapidly spread across the world. Karnataka's Home Minister G Parameshwara was quick to blame westernized clothing and behavior of young people. "They try to copy westerners not only in mindset, but even the dressing . . . some girls are harassed, these kind of things do happen," he said.

It is an all too familiar narrative. There is an enduring history of victim-blaming culture in India, from political elite through to convicted criminals.

In April 2015, during a political rally in the socially conservative state of Uttar Pradesh, former Chief Minister Mulayam Singh Yadav said in response to the conviction of gang rapists in Mumbai: "The poor fellows, three of them have been sentenced to death. Should rape cases lead to hanging? Boys are boys, they make mistakes."

In January 2014, Asha Mirje of the National Congress Party in Maharashtra said that "rapes take place also because of a woman's clothes, her behavior and her presence at inappropriate places." Congress colleagues distanced themselves from Mirje's remarks. She later apologized and said it is her personal view, not that of the party.

And how could we forget Mukesh Singh. Singh was the driver of the 2012 Delhi gang rape bus, where five men brutally raped Jyoti Singh, a 23-year-old physiotherapy student who later died of her injuries. When speaking to the BBC from Tihar Prison, Singh said that "a girl is far more responsible for rape than a boy. Boys and girls are not equal . . . About 20 percent of girls are good."

The list of examples goes on, and it exhaustively documented across the media. We are well acquainted with India's poor track record of women's safety. It is impossible to forget the horror of Jyoti Singh's gang rape. Since then, the safety of women in India has been under the microscope from domestic and international observers. The number of rapes reported in India has increased significantly, and the government has introduced new laws to fast track rape cases through the legal system.

India's Prime Minister Narendra Modi has attempted to find a solution to India's biggest PR problem. In May 2016, Modi declared that all mobile phones sold in India from 1 January 2017 must have a panic button. The theory behind the device is that when a woman is attacked, she will whip out her mobile phone and alert her five closest friends by pressing the "panic button." At the time of the announcement, much of the criticism focused on the practicality of such a button and its broader implementation.

Unsurprisingly, we are three weeks into the New Year and these panic button-enabled phones are not yet available for purchase. Poor implementation of other government policy is partly to blame. Demonetization of 500 and 1,000 rupee notes in India resulted in mobile manufacturers seeking an extension to the sale of old inventory, prior to taking the panic button enabled devices to market.

These public policy failures (coupled with pervasive gender discrimination and cultural norms) beg the question: what steps can we take to prevent atrocities such as the mass molestation of women in Bengaluru? It is not an easy question to answer. The 57th Commission on the Status of Women, which addressed the prevention of violence against women and girls, concluded that prevention requires both education programs and the participation of men.

While it is easy to look at India and exoticize its problem with women's safety, India is not alone in this predicament. Here in

Despite Media Depictions, Stranger Rape Is Much Less Common than Partner and Acquaintance Rape

The current rape being discussed by the media is the Punjab one, in which the chief minister Prakash Singh Badal's transport business is somehow implicated. Despite instances of sexual assault committed against women and girls of all ages, castes, social strata, geographical locations being reported by the media on an everyday basis (as opposed to the quantum of attention they may later receive), the image that a stranger commits rape persists in the collective imagination. However, if one bothers to make an informed opinion on sexual assault, the reality is the exact opposite. National Crime Records Bureau data consistently shows that in the majority of sexual assaults, the accused is known to the woman. This particular fact—that a rape accused usually knows his victim—is a blind spot for the media, and the debates in print or electronic media rarely focus on it, even though TV show panelists often mention it. When television news channels report rape, it is only the ones are more violent and barbaric which are given attention. As far as the national electronic media

Australia, Our Watch states that one woman per week on average is killed at the hands of their partner. One in five women has experienced sexual violence. However, the political elite of Australia have not publicly pointed the finger at women. In fact, both Tony Abbott and Malcolm Turnbull deplored Australia's domestic violence epidemic during their respective terms as prime minister.

Speaking with Amanda Vanstone on Radio National's Counterpoint, I optimistically said that there are signs of change in India. However, New Year's Eve in Bengaluru demonstrates that despite some increase in gender equality indicators, things are not changing fast enough. India and Australia both have a long road ahead to make progress on these significant challenges that impact such a large number of our populations. To address these

> are concerned, they perpetuate the myth that it is only strangers who prey on women in dark alleys, when in fact, these happen to be a small percentage in the range of sexual assaults on women. Coverage of all issues mentioned above is important, but what is required is much, much more, if we are as a society to understand the lives of women. For instance, the lives of girls who go to school mostly centre on going to school and returning straight home. Boys make many stops to look at the world around them before they reach home. And what does a girl see when she reaches home? Work: helping her mother cook, clean, and look after the younger siblings. If journalists can understand the difference in the way girls and boys are brought up, it would go a long way in understanding that sexual violence against women is at the extreme end of the problems women face. There are too many other problems, hidden to the world because nobody has bothered to ask women about them. It starts with little denials of freedom, and progresses to bigger ones, including the freedom to not have sex with your husband when you don't feel like it.
>
> **"Why does the media perpetuate the myth of 'stranger' rapes?," The News Minute, May 1, 2015.**

shared challenges there is an opportunity for Australia and India to collaborate. To do so, we need strong and consistent leadership from men and women; increased dialogue between policy makers and civil society; and accountability of public policy through measureable and publicly reported outcomes.

VIEWPOINT 2

> *"From the 20th century, in television, films, commercials, and music videos, sexualization and objectification of women became an increasingly growing trend."*

Girls and Women Are Exploited by the Media

Swagata Sen

In the following viewpoint Swagata Sen asserts that mainstream media has caused girls and women to be viewed as commodities through sexualization and objectification. Sen argues that this trend has negative impacts not only for young girls and women, but it also negatively affects boys by normalizing the dehumanization of women. The objectification of women has a detrimental impact on their mental and physical health and creates a culture in which girls and women are pressured to make their bodies conform to unrealistic standards in order to be desirable. Swagata Sen is a clinical researcher and advocate of women's rights and gender equality.

As you read, consider the following questions:

1. What industry grossly exploits girls and women, as reported by Sen?
2. What can justify violence against women, as stated by the author?

"Objectification and Exploitation of Girls and Women by the Mass Media and Social Media," by Swagata Sen, Rights of Equality, June 30, 2019. Reprinted with permission.

3. How does exploitation of girls and women affect boys, according to this viewpoint?

Objectification of Women by Media

Women and their bodies have always been commodities and sources of pleasure and exploitation for patriarchal cultures. From the 20th century, in television, films, commercials, and music videos, sexualization and objectification of women became an increasingly growing trend. Mainstream media has always used a false and unreal image of women's physical appearance, body image, behavioral standards and beauty. Today, across television, billboards, glossy pages of magazines, and social media we can see hypersexualized and unrealistically perfect female forms. Advertisements, music videos, and films dehumanize girls and women and portray them as commodities. Women's bodies are used to sell everything from car tires to entertainment. Read on this blog to know different forms of objectification of women by media and how that impacts our society.

Exploitation of Girls and Women by the Fashion Industry

Over the last 25 years, big clothing and cosmetic brands have started targeting young girls and women. The fashion industry hypersexualizes girls and women's clothing. Wearing tights, extremely short, or revealing dresses are characterized by boldness. Advertisements show them wearing highly provocative dresses, make-up, and often in age-inappropriate, hypersexualized postures and body language. Trying to keep up with the latest fashions, often kids and parents become victims of these brands. Models, supermodels, beauty queens, even dolls reinforce the idea that girls and women must have unrealistic beauty and figures. Fashion brands not only target women customers but also price girls' and women's products much higher than boys' and men's products. gender-based pricing is often referred to as the "Pink Tax." The

Pink Tax costs the average woman over $1,300 a year and impacts all aspects of daily life.

Sexual Objectification in Different Professions

There are many professions such as certain forms of dancing, beauty pageants, modeling, and cheerleading where women's objectification is encouraged and promoted. In addition, many women work in environments where the main purpose is to offer explicit targets for men to objectify them e.g., exotic dancing and cocktail waitressing.

Self-Objectification, Depression, and Self-Harm Among Young Girls and Women

Many studies have shown that media has negative effects on the mental health of young women and girls. Women perceive that their physical beauty is a measure of the amount of love and the power they should receive, putting tremendous pressure on them to conform to conventional beauty standards. According to psychologists, women internalize people's objectification of their bodies, resulting in them constantly criticizing their own bodies. Girls and women compulsively monitor their own body's outward appearance. They become overly concerned about how others may perceive their physical appearance.

According to Jess Wiener, the cultural expert for the Dove Self-Esteem Project, "Viewing unrealistic and unachievable beauty images creates an unattainable goal which leads to feelings of failure. This is especially true of young girls who have grown up in a world of filters and airbrushing."

Sense of Empowerment in Self-Objectification

Women in many western cultures participate in their own objectification, often without realizing it. This is the result of an increasing acceptance of the pornification of mainstream media in a culture that largely embraces materialism and objectification. Thus, many women actively consent to objectification and overt attempts to gain male attention by purposefully and consciously advertising their own object status. Girls and women who think they must wear revealing dresses to look beautiful are victims of patriarchy. But, when women need to use their bodies to draw the attention of the world, it is counterproductive to empowerment.

Normalizing Violence Against Women

According to UNICEF, "The objectification and sexualization of girls in the media is linked to violence against women and girls worldwide."

The media normalizes the act of dominance and aggression against women by constantly showcasing them as objects of pleasure. Boys and men tend to internalize that message, and it influences their subconscious biases of how they view women. They tend to legitimize violence, harassment, and anti-women views and behaviors.

Andrea Dworkin writes in her book *Woman Hating*, the process of turning women into sex objects is the first step towards justifying violence against them. Dworkin explains that if the media views women as a series of parts rather than a whole person, then inflicting violence upon them becomes easier to justify. Sandra Lee Bartky also describes sexual objectification as a form of dehumanization in her book *Femininity and Domination*. She explains that turning women into sex objects disciplines them into a state of submission. It teaches them to monitor their appearance and behaviors in order to suit harmful cultural norms. Sexual objectification is thus a way of denigrating women as a class.

Attitude of Boys Towards Girls and Relationship

Boys, from a very early age, are exposed to unrealistic, vulgar, hypersexualized images of women everywhere. The roles, and behaviors of women in films, music videos and commercials are too stereotypical and a far cry from equality. Along with objectifying women, glorified male masculinity, male dominance in media and mass media have deep impacts on shaping up a children's mind.

If a child is exposed to certain experiences as a part of his/her normal developmental dynamics, they tend to normalize it and develop a lot of unconscious biases towards that experience. These children would definitely grow up to replicate those experiences in their lives as adults.

Boys learn to dehumanize women and view them merely as bodies or body parts of pleasures. It causes mental health issues among boys and their unrealistic expectations from women. Women's sexuality and body interfere with their ability to have a healthy and functional relationship as adults.

Resources for Media Literacy and Media Activisms

Killing Us Softly is a documentary first released in 1979 and since revised and updated four times, focuses on images of women in advertising, in particular on gender stereotypes, the effects of advertising on women's self-image, and the objectification of women's bodies.

Studies suggested "the need for media literacy and media activism to help change the current normative body discontent of women in the Western world." We have seen a growing number of actresses, models, and feminists activists have started speaking against media and the internet for objectifying women.

4 Every Girl campaign is calling on entertainment and media industry leaders to create an environment where young girls feel valued and are defined by health media images of themselves. Sign their petition to call on leaders in the media to produce media images that respect, empower, and promote the true value of every girl.

Preventing Eating Disorders: A Handbook of Interventions and Special Challenges is a published book of the comprehensive resource provides multiple prevention strategies, programs, and approaches for health and mental health workers, educators, researchers, students, and interested members of the community at large who work to prevent eating disorders and related problems.

"Go Girls" (adapted from Giving Our Girls Inspiration and Resources for Lasting Self-esteem) program is a program that brings junior and senior high school girls together to advocate responsible advertising and positive body images of youth by the media.

The Geena Davis Institute on Gender in Media works within the media and entertainment industry to engage, educate and influence media producers to dramatically improve gender representation in films; to stop stereotyping girls and women; and to create diverse female characters in entertainment targeting children ages 11 and under.]

VIEWPOINT 3

> "If we can't talk about patriarchy, then let's admit that we are giving up on the idea of gender justice and goal of a world without rape."

A Culture of Patriarchy Leads to Rape Culture

Robert Jensen

In the following viewpoint Robert Jensen analyzes the culture of patriarchy and how it relates to sexual violence and rape culture, pointing out that it causes women to be viewed as sexual objects to be obtained. Jensen analyzes the patriarchal basis of rape, defines it, and explains that although only a very small percentage of men commit rape, there are other ways of participating in rape culture that more men engage in. While holding men who commit rape accountable is important, Jensen argues that a cultural shift is necessary to have a significant impact. Robert Jensen is a journalism professor at the University of Texas at Austin.

As you read, consider the following questions:

1. Who is most commonly committing rape, as reported by this author?
2. What is patriarchy, as explained by Jensen?
3. According to this viewpoint, how many U.S. women are rape survivors?

"Rape, rape culture and the problem of patriarchy," by Robert Jensen, Waging Nonviolence, April 29, 2014. Reprinted with permission.

How Does Culture Affect Sexual Consent?

By the end of Sexual Assault Awareness Month, two key questions were on the table for those who not only are aware of rape but would like to end men's violence against women.

First, do we live in a rape culture, or is rape perpetrated by a relatively small number of predatory men?

Second, is rape a clearly definable crime, or are there gray areas in sexual encounters that defy easy categorization as either consensual or non-consensual?

If those seem to be tricky, or trick, questions, don't worry. There's an easy answer to both: patriarchy (more on that shortly).

This year's Sexual Assault Awareness Month in April was full of the usual stories about men's violence, especially on university campuses. From football-obsessed state schools to elite private campuses, the reality of rape and rape culture was reported by journalists and critiqued by victim-survivors.

But April also included an unexpected debate within the anti-violence movement about the appropriate boundaries of the discussion about rape and rape culture.

"In the last few years, there has been an unfortunate trend towards blaming 'rape culture' for the extensive problem of sexual violence on campuses," wrote the Rape, Abuse and Incest National Network, or RAINN, in a letter offering recommendations to the White House Task Force to Protect Students from Sexual Assault. "While it is helpful to point out the systemic barriers to addressing the problem, it is important to not lose sight of a simple fact: rape is caused not by cultural factors but by the conscious decisions, of a small percentage of the community, to commit a violent crime."

RAINN expressed concern that emphasizing rape culture makes "it harder to stop sexual violence, since it removes the focus from the individual at fault, and seemingly mitigates personal responsibility for his or her own actions."

Feminists pushed back, pointing out that it shouldn't be difficult to hold accountable the individuals who commit acts legally defined as rape, while we also discuss how prosecuting rapists is made difficult by those who blame victims and make excuses for men's violence, all of which is related to the way our culture routinely glorifies other types of men's violence (war, sports and action movies) and routinely presents objectified female bodies to men for sexual pleasure (pornography, Hollywood movies and strip clubs).

Meanwhile, conservative commentators picked up on all this, using it as a club to condemn the always-demonizable feminists for their allegedly unfair treatment of men and allegedly crazy critique of masculinity.

I'm a man who doesn't believe feminists are unfair or crazy. In fact, I believe the only sensible way to understand these issues is through a feminist critique of—you guessed it—patriarchy.

Rape and Rape-Like Behavior

Before wading into the reasons we need feminism, let's consider a hypothetical:

A young man and woman are on a first date. The man decides early in the evening that he would like to have sexual intercourse and makes his attraction to her clear in conversation. He does not intend to force her to have sex, but he is assertive in a way that she interprets to mean that he "won't take no for an answer." The woman does not want to have sex, but she is uncertain of how he will react if she rejects his advance. Alone in his apartment—in a setting in which his physical strength means she likely could not prevent him from raping her—she offers to perform oral sex, hoping that will satisfy him and allow her to get home without a direct confrontation that could become too intense, even violent. She does not tell him what she is thinking, out of fear of how he may react. The man accepts the offer of oral sex, and the evening ends without conflict.

If that sex happened—and it's an experience that women have described (see *Flirting with Danger* by Lynn Phillips and the companion film)—should we describe the encounter as consensual sex or rape? In legal terms, this clearly is not rape. So, it's consensual sex. No problem, right?

Consider some other potentially relevant factors: If a year before that situation, the woman had been raped while on a date, would that change our assessment? If she had been sexually assaulted as a child and still, years later, goes into a survival mode when triggered? If this were a college campus and the man was a well-known athlete, and she feared the system would protect him?

By legal standards, this still clearly is not rape. But by human standards, this doesn't feel like fully consensual sex. Maybe we should recognize that both those assessments are reasonable. In short, rape is a definable crime that happens in a rape culture—once again, both things are true.

What Is Patriarchy and Why Does It Matter?

Patriarchy is a term rarely heard in mainstream conversation, especially since the backlash against feminism took off in the 1980s. So, let's start with the late feminist historian Gerda Lerner's definition of patriarchy as "the manifestation and institutionalization of male dominance over women and children in the family and the extension of male dominance over women in the society in general." Patriarchy implies, she continued, "that men hold power in all the important institutions of society and that women are deprived of access to such power. It does *not* imply that women are either totally powerless or totally deprived of rights, influence and resources."

Feminism challenges acts of male dominance and analyzes the underlying patriarchal ideology that tries to make that dominance seem inevitable and immutable. Second-wave radical feminists in the second half of the 20th century identified men's violence against women—rape, child sexual assault, domestic violence and various forms of harassment—as a key method of patriarchal control and made a compelling argument that sexual assault cannot be understood outside of an analysis of patriarchy's ideology.

Some of those feminists argued that "rape is about power not sex," but other feminists went deeper, pointing out that when women describe the range of their sexual experiences it becomes clear there

Social Influence and Sex

American parents often worry that their adolescent children are susceptible to their friends' influence and will be pressured into having sex before they are ready to do so. Are these worries justified?

Past research *has* found that social influence is associated with behaviors such as smoking and alcohol use among teenagers.[1,2] A recent study[3] extended this work and investigated whether three types of social influence predict adolescent sexual behavior:

1. **Peer pressure** refers to the explicit and direct social pressure to conform with the demands of a particular group to "fit in." In this case, adolescents might be motivated to have sex (or not) because they think they will be liked better by their friends, or disliked if they don't conform to the group (i.e., "C'mon, everyone's doing it").
2. **Thinking Your Friends Approve:** *Injunctive norms* are reflected in one's beliefs about others' attitudes towards a particular behavior. For example, an adolescent may believe that their friends approve or disapprove of having sex. The friends are not directly telling the teenager to have sex (that would be peer pressure, see above). Rather, injunctive norms operate indirectly; friends and classmates may simply make it known that they think having sex is okay (or not).
3. **Thinking Your Friends are Doing It:** *Descriptive norms* refer to what one believes others themselves are doing. If a teenager believes that their peers are having sex, then they may be more likely to also engage in sex as result of

is no bright-line distinction between rape and not-rape, but instead a continuum of sexual intrusion into women's lives by men. Yes, men who rape seek a sense of power, but men also use their power to get sex from women, sometimes under conditions that are not legally defined as rape but involve varying levels of control and coercion.

So, the focus shouldn't be reduced to a relatively small number of men who engage in behavior we can easily label as rape. Those men pose a serious problem and we should be diligent in prosecuting

> role modeling or imitation. Like injunctive norms, it is a less direct form of social influence than explicit peer pressure.
>
> The research team[3] combined the results from 58 independent studies conducted between 1980 and 2012, including almost 70,000 adolescents from 24 countries, using a statistical technique known as *meta-analysis*. By combining the results from many studies about a particular topic, the findings generated by a meta-analysis are powerful because they are relatively uninfluenced by statistical aberrations from a single study.
>
> Of the three types of social influence, descriptive norms had the largest association with adolescent sexual behavior. Injunctive norms were the next best predictor of teenage sex, and peer pressure was the weakest. In short, although parents may be worried about the effects of peer pressure on their teenage children, simply knowing about their friends' and classmates' own sexual behavior is likely a much more powerful force for adolescents.
>
> **Notes**
>
> [1] De Vries, H., Backbier, E., Kok, G., & Dijkstra, M. (1995). The impact of social influences in the context of attitude, self-efficacy, intention, and previous behavior as predictors of smoking onset. *Journal of Applied Social Psychology, 25*, 237-257.
> [2] Borsari, B., & Carey, K. B. (2003). Descriptive and injunctive norms in college drinking: A meta-analytic integration. *Journal of Studies on Alcohol, 64*, 331.
> [3] van de Bongardt, D., Reitz, E., Sandfort, T., & Dekovic, M. (in press). A meta-analysis of the relations between three types of peer norms and adolescent sexual behavior. *Personality and Social Psychology Review.* Online first.
> "Social Influence and Teen Sex: What Matters and What Doesn't," by Dr. Benjamin Le, Luvze, November 20, 2014.

them. But that prosecution can go on — and, in fact, will be aided by — recognizing the larger context in which men are trained to seek control and pursue conquest in order to feel like a man, and how that control is routinely sexualized.

Patriarchal Sex

If this seems far-fetched, think about the ways men in all-male spaces often talk about sex, such as asking each other, "Did you get any?" From that perspective, sex is the acquisition of pleasure from a woman, something one takes from a woman, and men talk openly among themselves about strategies to enhance the likelihood of "getting some" even in the face of resistance from women.

This doesn't mean that all men are rapists, that all heterosexual sex is rape or that egalitarian relationships between men and women are impossible. It does mean, however, that rape is about power *and* sex, about the way men are trained to understand ourselves and to see women.

Let me repeat: The majority of men do not rape. But consider these other categories:

- Men who do not rape but would be willing to rape if they were sure they would not be punished.
- Men who do not rape but will not intervene when another man rapes.
- Men who do not rape but buy sex with women who have been, or likely will be, raped in the context of being prostituted.
- Men who do not rape but will watch films of women in situations that depict rape or rape-like acts.
- Men who do not rape but find the idea of rape sexually arousing.
- Men who do not rape but whose sexual arousal depends on feeling dominant and having power over a woman.
- Men who do not rape but routinely masturbate to pornography in which women are presented as objectified bodies whose primary, or only, function is to provide sexual pleasure for men.

Those men are not rapists. But is that fact—that the men in these categories are not, in legal terms, guilty of rape—comforting? Are we advancing the cause of ending men's violence against women by focusing only on the acts legally defined as rape?

Rape Is Rape, and Rape Culture Is Rape Culture

Jody Raphael's book *Rape is Rape: How Denial, Distortion, and Victim Blaming Are Fueling a Hidden Acquaintance Rape Crisis* points out that if we use "a conservative definition of rape about which there can be no argument"—rape as an act of "forcible penetration"—the research establishes that between 10.6 percent and 16.1 percent of American women have been raped. That means somewhere between 12 million and 18 million women in this country today live as rape victim-survivors, if we use a narrow definition of the crime.

Because no human activity takes place in an ideological vacuum—the ideas in our heads affect the way we behave—it's hard to make sense of those numbers without the concept of rape culture. A rape culture doesn't command men to rape, but it does make rape inviting, and it reduces the likelihood rapists will be identified, arrested, prosecuted, convicted and punished. It's hard to imagine any meaningful efforts to reduce, and someday eliminate, rape without talking openly and honestly about these matters. But RAINN argues that such denial is exactly the path we should take.

Why should we fear talking about the socialization process by which boys and men are trained to see themselves as powerful over women and to see women as sexual objects? Why should we fear asking critical questions about all-male spaces, such as athletic teams and fraternities, where these attitudes might be reinforced? Could it be a fear that the problem of sexual assault is so deeply entwined in our taken-for-granted assumptions about gender that any serious response to the problem of rape requires us to all get more radical, to take radical feminism seriously?

This does not mean all men are rapists, that all male athletes are rapists, or that all fraternity members are rapists. It does mean that if we want to stop sexual violence, we have to confront patriarchy. If we decide we aren't going to talk about patriarchy, then let's stop pretending we are going to stop sexual violence and recognize that, at best, all we can do is manage the problem. If we can't talk about patriarchy, then let's admit that we are giving up on the idea of gender justice and goal of a world without rape.

It's easy to understand why people don't like this formulation of the problem, given that anything beyond a tepid liberal, postmodern feminism is out of fashion these days and radical feminist analyses of male dominance are rarely part of polite conversation. Sometimes people concede the value of such an analysis, but justify the silence about it by claiming, "People can't handle it." When someone makes that claim, I assume what they mean is "I can't handle it myself," that it's too much, too painful to deal with.

That's not hard to understand, because to confront the reality of rape and rape culture is to realize that vigorous prosecution of the small number of men who rape doesn't solve the larger problem.

If anyone still doubts that rape culture exists and is relevant, how else would we explain the Yale University fraternity members who marched on campus while shouting sexist chants, including "No means yes, yes means anal," as part of a 2010 pledge event?

Everyone recognizes the mocking reference to the anti-rape message, "No means no," which expresses women's demand that men listen to them. These Yale men reject that. The second part of their chant—"Yes means anal"—states that women who agree to sex are implicitly agreeing to anything a man wants, including anal penctration. This will make sense to anyone who is aware of the prevalence of anal penetration in today's pornography marketed to heterosexual men. In those pornographic scenes, women sometimes beg for that penetration and other times are forced into it, but the message is the same: Men's pleasure is central.

In this one chant, these men of Yale—one of the most elite universities in the United States, which produces some of the country's most powerful business and political leaders, including five presidents—clearly express a patriarchal view of gender and sex. Their chant is an endorsement of rape and an expression of rape culture.

Is a feminist critique of rape and rape culture a threat to me as a man? I was socialized in a patriarchal culture to believe that whatever feminists had planned, I should be afraid of it. But what I have learned from radical feminists is that quite the opposite is true—feminism is a gift to men. Such critique does not undermine my humanity, but instead gives me a chance to embrace it.

VIEWPOINT 4

> "Girls and women have been using digital media technologies to challenge rape culture and sexual violence."

The #MeToo Movement Brings Sexual Assault Out in the Open

Jessalynn Keller

In the following viewpoint Jessalynn Keller analyzes social media movements like #MeToo and how these digital platforms affect the survivors of sexual assault. Keller outlines how important digital platforms become to survivors by allowing them to give voice to their personal experiences while also enabling them to connect with other survivors. The #MeToo campaign and similar campaigns both make the issue of sexual assault more personal and demonstrate how widespread it is. In doing so, it has helped raise feminist consciousness. Jessalynn Keller is a professor of critical media studies at the University of Calgary in Alberta, Canada.

As you read, consider the following questions:

1. What is "hashtag feminism" as explained in this viewpoint?

"#MeToo campaign brings conversation of rape to the mainstream", by Jessalynn Keller, The Conversation, October 24, 2017. https://theconversation.com/metoo-campaign-brings-conversation-of-rape-to-the-mainstream-85875. Licensed under CC BY-ND 4.0 International.

2. How do women use hashtag feminism to fight back against rape culture, according to Keller?
3. Does digital sharing of sexual assault stories help survivors, according to the author?

The first #MeToo appeared unexpectedly in my Facebook feed about 10 days ago, a digital response by girls and women to the allegations of sexual harassment and violence against Hollywood producer Harvey Weinstein. Using the #MeToo hashtag, girls and women publicly identified that they too have experienced sexual assault.

Soon, my social media accounts were flooded with the hashtag and accompanying stories of sexual harassment and violence that seemed to mark the lives of nearly all of my female friends and acquaintances. According to the Associated Press, the hashtag was shared in more than 12 million Facebook posts and reactions in the first 24 hours.

I am still moved by these stories, despite having spent the past three years studying similar testimonials with my co-researchers — Kaitlynn Mendes at the University of Leicester and Jessica Ringrose at the University College of London's Institute of Education. We have been exploring the ways in which girls and women have been using digital media technologies to challenge rape culture and sexual violence.

We spoke to over 50 girls and women primarily based in Canada, the United States and the United Kingdom who had engaged in such practices. Some had used the hashtag #BeenRapedNeverReported to share experiences of sexual violence in the wake of the Jian Ghomeshi allegations, while others posted their stories of street harassment on websites like Hollaback!.

Women told us how they confronted rape jokes on Facebook. Some spoke of launching social media campaigns that addressed their own sexual assaults. #MeToo is not an isolated incident then, but part of a trajectory of digital feminist consciousness raising that is making rape culture visible within mainstream culture.

Feminist Politics in the Digital Age

Over the past week there has been excellent commentary on #MeToo, including intersectional critiques of the hashtag, conversations about the need to name perpetrators and exploration of the roots of the movement.

I do not want to repeat these important analyses here (although I recommend reading them), but instead draw on our research to consider what #MeToo offers the girls and women who used the hashtag this past week, and what the hashtag suggests about contemporary feminist politics in the digital age.

While some are doubtful about the potential for hashtags like #MeToo to produce social change, our research findings indicate that "hashtag feminism" can help to bring about feminist consciousness and solidarity that is an imperative step towards a more equitable society.

Social Media: The Power of Personal Narratives

Hashtags like #MeToo are one of the strategies that have been used by survivors of sexual violence and harassment, functioning as a way to make their voices heard through personal story, while connecting to others with similar experiences.

Over the past five years, several hashtags have been mobilized for such a purpose, including #YesAllWomen, #YouOkSis? and #BeenRapedNeverReported.

The latter served as one of the case studies in our research. In addition to analyzing hundreds of #BeenRapedNeverReported tweets, we also interviewed girls and women who had used the hashtag to share stories about why they didn't report their sexual assaults.

To anyone who thinks that women quickly and absentmindedly tweet these types of stories—you couldn't be more wrong. The girls and women we spoke with described painful debates with themselves over whether they should post about their sexual assaults, sleepless nights thinking about the consequences and anxiety that upon tweeting, as one participant put it, "no one would notice."

The Double Bind of Hashtags: Triggering and Comforting

Another participant described the weeks in late 2014, when the #BeenRapedNeverReported trended, as being "absolutely gut-wrenching." She said:

> It was very emotional and it was very upsetting to me, this whole thing, being a part of that hashtag, reading other women's little tweets, 140-character tweets. One resonated and it was really a tough couple of weeks. Even though it was positive, it was very, very difficult for me. There were some nights where I didn't sleep.

Comments like this highlight the double bind that survivors find themselves in when hashtags like #BeenRapedNeverReported or #MeToo trend; they can be simultaneously triggering and comforting. As hashtags like #MeToo attract wide audiences, we need to recognize that these responses exist together in the complex terrain of hashtag feminism.

Yet, the women we spoke with also talked about the significant support they received upon tweeting about their assaults. One woman told us:

> I got an overwhelming awesome response the night I posted... There was one... all she said was, 'we stand with you, friend.' And that one made me cry. I'll admit it, that one made me cry. And then there was one that told me I was incredibly strong and brave for doing what I did.... there was six or seven comments like that. Which, for me, was overwhelming because I didn't really think that anyone would say these things, you know, it was just I was helping the hashtag understand why things weren't being reported. And I didn't really expect any response at all. And next thing you know, I got likes and favorites and comments, and I was just, like, oh, my gosh, what is going on here.

This woman's experience is indicative of many of the girls and women we spoke to; they emphasized being pleasantly surprised by the comments, retweets and "favorites" they received from strangers online and how these seemingly small responses—a click of the Twitter heart icon or a brief comment—came to mean so much.

We cannot dismiss the significance of this. Indeed, if hashtags like #BeenRapedNeverReported and #MeToo are making survivors feel heard as our participant describes above, then they are worthwhile, regardless if Harvey Weinstein works again or not.

Raising Feminist Consciousness

We also discovered that sharing stories via social media often generates feminist consciousness that is needed for structural change. For example, another one of our interviewees told us that she began to identify as a feminist only after sharing her story of sexual assault on social media.

Digital sharing allowed her to link her own experience to that of thousands of other girls and women and recognize that sexual violence was a structural problem, rather than an individual experience. Another young woman who was assaulted on a university campus described to us how tweeting about her experience was the important first step in reporting the assault to the authorities. She said:

> For me, [sharing my story with the #BeenRapedNeverReported hashtag] was kind of the strength to say I can report this. And so it gave me the option and the power to actually go through to campus security . . . I'm not sure if it was because I finally put my name to it [the assault] or because I had seen so many other stories. There was a solidarity with it where I felt comfortable and ready to.

Of course, girls and women should never be obligated to share their traumatic stories in order to believed; several people have written about that in relation to #MeToo.

However, our interviews do point to the opportunities for feminist consciousness and solidarity that hashtags like

#BeenRapedNeverReported and #MeToo provide, especially for girls and women who may be unfamiliar with feminist politics and unlikely to identify with the movement.

These shifts in consciousness may go unnoticed at first, but over time this "mainstreaming" of feminist activism is the foundation for the creation of a more just society.

Within this optimistic and celebratory argument of the power of social media to produce social change, we still recognize that social media platforms like Twitter and Facebook profit from trending hashtags, accumulating large amounts of personal data to sell to advertisers.

We must then grapple with the question of what it means for digital feminist consciousness raising and solidarity to be intimately connected to the digital capitalism promoted by the tech sector—one of the most sexist industries today.

VIEWPOINT 5

> "There are many hurdles to male sexual abuse survivors receiving needed mental health care. When encountering perceived authority figures, such as health care providers, these men sometimes experience harsh judgment and distrust."

Women Are Not the Only Victims of Sexual Assault and Abuse

Joan M. Cook and Amy Ellis

In this viewpoint Joan M. Cook and Amy Ellis discuss the psychiatric stress found in boys and men who have experienced sexual abuse, many of whom are in the LGBTQ+ community. They point out that sexual abuse is much more common among men than most people expect and that many of these men do not seek out help because they're afraid of being stigmatized or experiencing victim-blaming. LGBTQ+ men face the additional challenge of being a sexual or gender minority, which often compounds the psychological impacts of sexual abuse. In order to help curb this culture of sexual abuse among men and LGBTQ+ individuals, the public and health care workers need to become better informed about this issue. Joan M. Cook is a professor in the department of psychiatry at the Yale School of Medicine. Amy Ellis is the Assistant Director of the Trauma

"Sexual Abuse Against Gay and Bi Men Brings Unique Stigma and Harm," by Joan M. Cook and Amy Ellis, The Conversation, August 29, 2019, https://theconversation.com/sexual-abuse-against-gay-and-bi-men-brings-unique-stigma-and-harm-121796. Licensed under CC BY-ND 4.0 International.

Resolution & Integration Program at Nova Southeastern University, where she is also an assistant clinical professor.

As you read, consider the following questions:

1. What health disparities are faced by gay and bisexual men who experience sexual abuse?
2. What is minority stress, according to this viewpoint?
3. What factors may lead men to not seek help after experiencing sexual abuse, according to this viewpoint?

As trauma psychologists, we're leading a team to help alleviate psychiatric distress in gay, bi and trans males who have been sexually abused or assaulted. In collaboration with two nonprofit organizations, MaleSurvivor and Men Healing, we recruited and trained 20 men who have experienced sexual abuse to deliver evidence-based online mental health interventions for sexual and gender minority males—an umbrella term for individuals whose sexual identity, orientation or practices differ from the majority of society.

This study should help men in this group who have been sexually assaulted know that they are not alone, that they are not to blame for their abuse, and that healing is possible.

But, there are some things that trauma psychologists already know about these men, such as how prevalent sexual abuse of men is and ways to help men recover.

All Too Common, All Too Traumatic

At least 1 in 6 boys are sexually abused before their 18th birthday. This number rises to 1 in 4 men across their lifespan.

The rates of sexual abuse and assault are even higher in boys and men from sexual minority populations.

Sexual violation in gay, bisexual, transgender and intersex individuals often complicates their sense of self, and how they fit, or don't fit, into LGBTQ+ culture and communities. Such abuse may even impact their reaching out for help or reporting traumatic events as they fear stigmatization or victim-blaming.

Men and women who have experienced sexual abuse and assault are at risk for a wide range of medical, behavioral and sexual disorders. They have high rates of several psychiatric disorders, including post-traumatic stress disorder, substance abuse and dependence, depression and anxiety, as well as greater risk for suicide. They also have more educational, occupational and interpersonal difficulties than non-abused men. Further, sexual trauma is linked to medical illnesses, increased health care utilization and poor quality of life.

But, sexual minority males who have experienced sexual trauma face even greater health disparities. Gay and bisexual men with histories of childhood and adult sexual victimization are more likely to report greater numbers of sexually transmitted infections, increased sexual risk for human immunodeficiency virus, and higher sexual compulsivity than men with no history of sexual assault. In addition, sexual minority male survivors exhibit more negative psychological outcomes related to their sexual identities, such as lower self-esteem, distorted sense of self and difficulties forming healthy adult intimate relationships.

The cumulative impact of sexual abuse, in conjunction with individuals' sexual minority status, also can result in higher rates of sexual re-victimization, as well as anti-gay violence and discrimination.

Discrimination Galore

Gay and bisexual men are also exposed to significant minority stress, a term used to describe the sociopolitical stressors placed on individuals as a result of their minority status. Sexual orientation disparities start relatively early in development. LGBTQ+ individuals are disproportionately exposed to day-to-day discrimination, peer and parental rejection, unsupportive or hostile work or social environments, and unequal access to opportunities afforded to heterosexuals, including marriage, adoption and employment nondiscrimination.

Chronic expectations of rejection, internalized homophobia, alienation and lack of integration with the community can understandably lead to problems with self-acceptance. As a result, a sexual minority male who has experienced sexual abuse may feel deficient, inferior or impaired. Further, they may view themselves as shameful, undesirable, undeserving, or incapable of forming a loving relationship.

Many sexual minority males who have experienced sexual abuse internalize harmful beliefs that make it harder for them to heal. These myths include the false belief that men cannot be forced to have sex against their will; that men who become sexually aroused or have an erection when assaulted must have wanted or enjoyed it; and that real men should welcome any opportunity to have sex.

These men often bottle up additional detrimental myths, such as men become gay or bisexual because they were sexually abused, and sexual minority men are obsessed with sex, and that they molest children at higher rates than straight men. Sexual minority males who have been abused are not born with these beliefs. They learn them from their families, religion, society and the media. But, the more men hold these beliefs to be true, the harder it is for them to move forward in their psychological recovery.

Getting the Help to Heal

These men typically do not seek formal mental health treatment. Or they take, on average, decades to do so. This is consistent with research on predictors of engagement in mental health services in the larger population, as well as in those recovering from trauma. In general, men seek mental health assistance at lower rates than women. Similarly, in survivors of a broad range of traumatic events with post-traumatic stress disorder, decreased mental health service use was related to being male.

Additionally, despite similar rates of military sexual trauma in men and women, men are less likely to seek and utilize professional help. Men are even less prone to seeking counseling when they have been most severely assaulted through penetration.

There are many hurdles to male sexual abuse survivors receiving needed mental health care. When encountering perceived authority figures, such as health care providers, these men sometimes experience harsh judgment and distrust. In addition, when initiating psychological services, they may have difficulty finding knowledgeable and experienced health care providers who understand the nuances specific to male sexual abuse and, consequently, won't disclose their sexual trauma.

Nondisclosure of sexual abuse may also be due to a male's own lack of understanding of what abuse is. This is in line with research that found that the majority of men who endorsed survey items or behaviors indicating sexual abuse did not actually label themselves as sexual abuse survivors. Not disclosing one's sexual trauma history is associated with increased emotional distress, while self-disclosure and seeking mental health services are related to psychological well-being.

VIEWPOINT 6

> "Considering gender inequality is a well-known driver of domestic violence and abuse, peddling women's subordination as being ordained by God is placing the safety of conservative Christian women at risk."

How Religion Can Prevent Sexual Consent

Vicki Lowik and Annabel Taylor

In the following viewpoint Vicki Lowik and Annabel Taylor analyze the topic of sexual abuse and mistreatment from a religious standpoint. Lowik and Taylor maintain that evangelical Christian churches promote the acceptance and normalization of sexual abuse because of the beliefs that they preach. Lowik and Taylor look at the ways in which certain religious communities promote male authority and the ways this can lead to sexual and domestic violence. Vicki Lowik is a research assistant at the Queensland Center for Domestic and Family Violence at CQUniversity in Australia. Annabel Taylor is an assistant professor at the CQUniversity.

"Evangelical churches believe men should control women. That's why they breed domestic violence," by Vicki Lowik and Annabel Taylor, The Conversation, December 8, 2019. https://theconversation.com/evangelical-churches-believe-men-should-control-women-thats-why-they-breed-domestic-violence-127437. Licensed under CC BY-ND 4.0 International.

How Does Culture Affect Sexual Consent?

As you read, consider the following questions:

1. According to the authors, which church community is rife with abuse?
2. What is the reason behind abuse in the evangelical Christian community, as reported in this viewpoint?
3. Is there a way to change the toxic culture in the evangelical Christian church, according to Lowik and Taylor?

Jane* was a member of Australia's evangelical Christian community, and throughout her marriage she heard many sermons on honoring a husband's authority.

These sermons focused on a wife submitting to her husband's authority in everything, from finances to where and when she worked. He was to be respected as head of the family, because this was "God's plan."

For three decades, Jane's husband abused her under the guise of this notion of authority. He isolated her, denied her money and the use of a car. He yelled at her, kicked and punched her, told her she was mad and threatened to kill her.

Jane is a case study participant in my research, and she told me that when she went to her church leaders for support, they asked her what *she* was doing wrong. When she attempted to escape the abuse after the first decade of marriage, they told her to continue attending church with her husband.

Then, they told her to move back into the family home and resolve her marital issues, and that this would be the last time they gave her counselling on the matter.

Jane's story is a familiar one—an ABC investigation last year showed how conservative Christian churches both enable and conceal domestic violence.

My ongoing research shows this is exacerbated by what's taught in evangelical church communities, creating fertile ground for domestic violence, its justification and its concealment.

A Literal Reading of the Bible

Evangelical Christians believe biblical scripture is "truth" that "requires our unreserved submission in all areas of life." They consider scripture to be "inspired by the Holy Spirit," so "it is the supreme and final authority on all matters on which it speaks."

The effect of evangelical Christianity on women's vulnerability to domestic violence is yet to be measured through a comprehensive survey in Australia. But the extensive reporting on domestic violence in the evangelical Sydney Anglican Diocese challenges harmful and stubborn attitudes that place religious doctrine over the safety of women.

This resistance to cultural change is also shown by teachings on the permanence of the marriage covenant, another way women are potentially trapped in violent marriages.

A Backlash Against 1980s Christian Feminism

In the 1980s, Christian feminists began to challenge the exclusivity of male leadership in the church, as well as aspects of theology, including the assumption God was masculine in nature.

The feminist movement that had been gaining momentum in wider society during the 1960s and 1970s underpinned this revolt against male privilege in the church.

In fervent response, evangelical factions of the Christian church began to double down on men's authority over women.

In fact, evangelical Christian leaders who believed in the infallibility of biblical scripture, began to blame Christian feminists for creating more divorce, sexual abuse and promiscuity.

This backlash resulted in a renewed call for women to stop any resistance to their husband's authority, a call still echoing almost 40 years later.

Male Authority in God's Plan

Traditional understandings about male headship, both in the family and the Church, were promoted as being ordained by God. This meant the authority of men and the subordination of women were considered to be "permanently binding" principles.

Conservative evangelical Christians enthusiastically embraced this as a form of resistance against the feminist movement, and still support these "permanently binding" principles today.

Sadly, there are no statistics on the prevalence of domestic violence in the Australian Christian community, but it's addressed in international research. More Australian research is needed urgently.

In a survey of churchgoers in Cumbria, England, one in four respondents had experienced at least one of the nominated abusive behaviors—such as being kicked, punched, threatened with a weapon, isolated or sexually coerced—in their current relationship. And more than 40% of respondents had experienced at least one in a current or previous relationship.

The researchers noted evangelical churches were reluctant to participate in the survey, perhaps indicating the reluctance of these churches to address domestic violence in their own communities.

According to research carried out in North America, the rates of domestic violence in evangelical communities is considered to be at least as high as rates in other churches. But other U.S. research conducted a few years later suggests the rate could be even higher in evangelical churches because they are more likely to create an environment endorsing gender inequality.

Considering gender inequality is a well-known driver of domestic violence and abuse, peddling women's subordination as being ordained by God is placing the safety of conservative Christian women at risk.

Changing a Toxic Culture

The culture of male privilege in evangelical Christian communities can be changed with more women positioned as senior ministers. This move can disrupt notions that men have authority over women, and mean problems that affect women might no longer be overlooked.

These communities can also benefit from more education to understand that violence, with visible injuries, isn't the only form of domestic abuse. If church leaders and their congregations can recognize abuse in all its forms, they can take more appropriate steps to offer support to victims.

Most importantly, congregations benefit from hearing sermons that admonish domestic violence and advise victims to seek support and prioritize their safety, rather than sermons demanding women obey their husbands even in abusive circumstances. This would help stop Christian perpetrators using the Bible as an excuse for their behavior.

When perpetrators use their Christian beliefs to justify abuse, women like Jane are not only facing long-term physical and mental harm, but they are being denied a spiritual journey that can bring peace and friendship within a like-minded community.

*Names have been changed to protect privacy.

Periodical and Internet Sources Bibliography

The following articles have been selected to supplement the diverse views presented in this chapter.

Julia Baird and Hayley Gleeson, "Submit to Your Husbands: Women Told to Endure Domestic Violence in the Name of God," ABC, July 17, 2017. https://www.abc.net.au/news/2017-07-18/domestic-violence-church-submit-to-husbands/8652028.

Jess Hill, "Patriarchy and Power: How Socialisation Underpins Abusive Behavior," the *Guardian*, March 7, 2020. https://www.theguardian.com/society/2020/mar/08/patriarchy-and-power-how-gender-inequality-underpins-abusive-behaviour.

Katie McCoy, "God Is Not Silent: What the Bible Teaches About Sexual Assault," The Ethics and Religious Liberty Commission of the Southern Baptist Convention, December 11, 2017. https://erlc.com/resource-library/articles/god-is-not-silent-what-the-bible-teaches-about-sexual-assault/.

Elizabeth Nash, Leah H. Keller, and Sophia Naide, "State and Federal Lawmakers Promote Sexual Consent, LGBTQ+ Inclusivity in Sex Education," Guttmacher Institute, May 2019. https://www.guttmacher.org/article/2019/05/state-and-federal-lawmakers-promote-sexual-consent-lgbtq-inclusivity-sex-education.

Nancy E. Nienhuis, "Faith in the Face of Abuse," Harvard Divinity Bulletin, Spring/Summer 2009. https://bulletin.hds.harvard.edu/faith-in-the-face-of-abuse/.

Sheikh Saaliq, "Gang Rape of a Tourist in India Highlights Its Struggle to Curb Sexual Violence Against Women," AP World News, March 5, 2024. https://apnews.com/article/india-sexual-violence-rape-b9016c82074c08583080db846d64055b.

David Sanchez, "The Biblical Principles Behind Reporting Sexual Abuse," Texas Baptists, September 9, 2021. https://www.texasbaptists.org/article/the-biblical-principles-behind-reporting-sexual-abuse.

Michael Segalov, "Why Hasn't the Gay Community Had a #MeToo Moment?" the *Guardian*, March 7, 2018. https://www.theguardian.com/commentisfree/2018/mar/07/gay-community-metoo-moment-conversation-consent-sexual-assault.

Kamayani Sharma, "#MeToo: Understanding Consent and Sex-Positivity in a Patriarchal Society," Firstpost, November 17, 2018. https://www.firstpost.com/long-reads/metoo-understanding-consent-and-sex-positivity-in-a-patriarchal-society-5535191.html.

Zawn Villines, "Can Women Really Consent to Sex in a Patriarchal Society?" Liberating Motherhood, October 19, 2023. https://zawn.substack.com/p/can-women-really-consent-to-sex-in.

Megha Wadhwa, "Why Is India Failing to Protect Its Women?" the *Japan Times*, March 15, 2024. https://www.japantimes.co.jp/commentary/2024/03/15/world/india-sexual-violence-rape-roots/.

CHAPTER 3

Is Sex Work Consensual?

Chapter Preface

Despite its prevalence, sex work has long been stigmatized, and up until recently the legalization or decriminalization of it would likely not have received much support from the public. However, a report by the American Civil Liberties Union and the National Center for Transgender Equality finds that over 50 percent of Americans and two-thirds of voters aged 18 to 44 agree that sex work should be decriminalized.

While many people in the past (and even today) are morally opposed to sex work, others have begun to accept that it is simply another line of work, and one that can offer a lifeline to people who would be unable to make ends meet otherwise. However, research indicates that these individuals often experience violence and are at great risk of exposure to a number of diseases. This doesn't have to be the case. There are ways to end the life-threatening challenges faced by sex workers. Many might judge sex workers because they feel this work is immoral. Politicians may skirt the issue fearing constituents would judge them unworthy for office if they supported laws to aid this work. But many argue that sex work is work and that these workers need protections that other workers have.

This chapter's viewpoints cast a spotlight on these issues, looking at the arguments made by those who view sex work as a threat to society and the individuals who engage in it that must be controlled, as well as those who view sex workers as people who have made the decision to be employed in a high-risk industry and deserve protections they are not currently receiving.

VIEWPOINT 1

> *"For anti-trafficking campaigners, sex work is not work—it is exploitation. It is servitude. Even rape and sex work become synonymous for anti-trafficking activists because no women could ever choose it."*

Sex Work Is Often Considered Sex Slavery

Carly Daniel-Hughes

In this viewpoint Carly Daniel-Hughes discusses how Evangelical women have campaigned against human trafficking—specifically sex trafficking—and how they have shaped public conversation and policy on sex work by conflating sex work with sex trafficking. According to the organizations these women create, it is not possible for women to consent to sex work, as they consider it a form of servitude they are forced into. These organizations have joined forces with secular anti-prostitution feminists to prevent the decriminalization of sex work. Daniel-Hughes suggests that the motivation behind these campaigns may be to preserve the societal role of Protestant women as protectors of morality. Carly Daniel-Hughes is an associate professor of religious and cultural studies, gender and sexuality, and the history of Christianity at Concordia University in Montreal, Canada.

"Evangelical Women Are Shaping Public Attitudes About Sex Work," by Carly Daniel-Hughes, The Conversation, January 3, 2018, https://theconversation.com/evangelical-women-are-shaping-public-attitudes-about-sex-work-89129. Licensed under CC BY-ND 4.0 International.

As you read, consider the following questions:

1. Why does Daniel-Hughes say the relationship between secular feminist groups and Evangelical anti-trafficking organizations is a "surprising affiliation"?
2. What are some of the criticisms of anti-trafficking campaigns mentioned in this viewpoint?
3. What reason does Daniel-Hughes offer for the influence Evangelical anti-trafficking organizations has over sex work public policy?

Evangelical speaker and activist Christine Caine wants you to know: "Slavery still exists." Her organization A-21, which aims to abolish "injustice in the 21st century," says human trafficking affects 27 million people each year and is a $150 billion criminal industry.

Caine is on a mission to eradicate human trafficking. Stories of missing women and girls abducted in Europe and sold into the sex trade ignited her outrage and motivated her and her husband Nick Caine, an evangelical pastor, to launch the organization a decade ago. A-21 now works with law enforcement in 11 countries, including the United States and the United Kingdom, and provides safe houses where girls and women can be rehabilitated.

Caine is quick to tell her audiences the atrocities victims of trafficking have suffered. Girls are treated like livestock. They are crammed into shipping containers, some drown at sea; they are moved forcibly across borders; locked in apartments and brothels; made to have abortions, or "they give birth and the babies are sold into pedophile rings." These girls "are raped 20 maybe 30 times every day," says Caine.

These are gripping stories. And Caine's talks engage audiences with gruesome details, and then end on a high note. Every girl that is "saved" is given a new life. She is made free. This is a classic Protestant redemption story.

Dominating the Sex Work Debate

While Caine speaks about human trafficking, in fact, sex trafficking is her primary target, and with it the sex industry. In this, Caine is not alone. She represents a powerful constituency of conservative Christians who have formed non-profits of their own, such as FAAST, Wellspring Living and Concerned Women for America, and made alliances with anti-prostitution, secular feminists.

It is a surprising affiliation. In the U.S. in particular, secular feminists and conservative women have usually found themselves on opposite sides of social issues. For four decades they have been embattled over women's rights and abortion, as historian Marjorie Spurill has noted.

Yet evangelical women and anti-trafficking feminists come together on this point: the sale of sex threatens a woman's very humanity. And these groups dominate public discussion of sex work. They have, and continue to influence policy-making and legal enforcement of anti-sex-trafficking laws despite vehement criticisms by sex worker rights activists and their supporters.

The public debate about the sex trade finds sex workers unable to seek legal rights and protections on their own terms. Sex work, according to anthropologist Laura Maria Agustin, is very often an intelligible response made by women, men and trans-people to social, economic and political realities; it is strategic equation for many who engage in it. Their attitudes about the work vary. They do not always "like" their job. They would not deny that it can be dangerous (though the dangers are magnified when their labor is criminalized).

Yet for anti-trafficking campaigners, sex work is not work—it is exploitation. It is servitude. Even rape and sex work become synonymous for anti-trafficking activists because no women could ever *choose* it. The only solution, they say, is for women to leave the industry: to be saved or reformed.

Even "the most seemingly benign 'rehabilitation' programs for sex workers," writes Melissa Gira Grant in *Playing the Whore: The*

Work of Sex Work, "may be described as shelters, but the doors are locked, the phones are monitored, and guests are forbidden ... This isn't charity. This is control."

Criticisms of Anti-Trafficking Campaigns

Critics of these anti-trafficking campaigns have argued that the numbers of trafficked people put forward are inflated, or entirely unsubstantiated. They have asked whether most coerced labor is actually made of up trafficked women and girls, as the campaigns claim.

Sex-worker rights advocates and scholars have rejected the conflation of sex trafficking and prostitution that animates much anti-trafficking crusades, Christian and otherwise. For instance, Donna Hughes, an activist who helped to inform the Bush administration's anti-trafficking legislation, asserted that most of what people see as prostitution is "actually trafficking because it involves force, fraud and coercion or underage girls."

In fact, studies of sex workers even in sites of "sex tourism" (notably Cambodia) have not revealed large scale sex-trafficking rings. But what chance do such studies have in the face of the moral panic promoted by anti-traffickers?

The rhetoric of evangelical anti-trafficking activists, like Hughes and Caine, is sensationalist. Yet it works to incite fear, prurient interest, and a sense of moral righteousness. It is, explains scholar and sex worker rights advocate, Jo Doezma, evocative of the fabricated "white slave panic" of the 19th century that in its own day facilitated draconian measures against prostitutes and other working class women.

Why, we should ask, has it caught the moral imagination of evangelical communities and, particularly, evangelical women?

Why Anti-Trafficking Campaigns Attract Evangelical Women

One historic reason that drew evangelicals generally to the cause of anti-trafficking occurred during the Bush administration (2001-

2009). Bush established the Office of Faith-Based Initiatives, giving conservative Christian organizations new access to federal funds for their charitable work. Under Bush, however, anti-trafficking initiatives also became government policy. The Trump administration, too, may be investing in the issue.

In the last two decades, the fight against human trafficking has become something of an evangelical mission. One now finds fundraising walks , prayer weekends, Bible studies, self-help books and even praise songs devoted to ending global slavery.

Political factors alone did not draw evangelical women to anti-sex-trafficking crusades, however. So did the crusades' rhetoric, which is grounded in values that resonate deeply with conservative Protestant sexual morality.

A traditional script of sexual and gender roles is foundational to anti-trafficking activism. Girls are rehabilitated so that they can occupy their true positions as women, that is, as married women and mothers.

This is ultimately what anti-trafficking activists mean by freedom, Yvonne Sherman argues in *Other Dreams of Freedom: Religion, Sex, and Human Trafficking*. This notion of freedom is entirely commensurate with conservative Protestant views of sexuality—initially articulated by the 16th century reformers, Martin Luther and John Calvin, who championed marriage and rejected celibacy and monasticism.

Following their teachings, conservative Protestants have argued that marriage alone is the appropriate sexual relationship, divinely ordained. It is the only one that ensures a proper relationship with God. As such, sexual relations outside of marriage are imagined as bondage. Here, then, we see how sex work can readily become sex slavery.

But there is more: Evangelical women can see themselves as uniquely suited to this particular cause because of its moral tenor. Conservative Protestant women have a long history of fashioning themselves as guardians of the moral order, more specifically of marriage and the family, a strategy they have employed to legitimate

THE REALITIES OF SEX TRAFFICKING

Those who are sex trafficked often come to be victims in one of two ways. They are forced or coerced into nonconsensual sexual behaviors or positions of sexual exploitation, or they enter willingly into occupations, such as prostitution or acting in adult films, and later are forced or coerced into non-consensual situations (Burke, 2013). In a forthcoming study of mine, I interviewed a variety of women about their experiences in the adult film industry. Several of these women discussed having willingly entered the industry and it was only after they became embedded in the business of adult film did, they report being manipulated or forced to engage in sexual behaviors in which they did not want to participate. But sex workers are far from the only demographic of people that can become victims of sex trafficking.

Characteristics of Sex Trafficking Victims

There is a wide array of characteristics and group inclusions that make up the demographics of those who are sex trafficked. Sex trafficking victims can include:

- Persons of any sex or gender
- Pregnant women and LGBTQ+ youth are at a high risk for sex trafficking based on the increased money traffickers can make from these groups
- Youth in the foster care system

their political and social campaigns, from suffrage and temperance to abortion and same-sex marriage debates.

Trafficked women are victims in need of saving, evangelical anti-trafficking activists proclaim. The labor that evangelicals undertake to do so is arduous. Caine warns: few will be rescued, only 1 percent. Her assertion, however, is not self-defeating. It compels her audience to action, by playing on an apocalyptic scenario that amplifies the testimonial power of one "saved" victim, and so, too, her heroic saviors.

- Persons with mental health issues
- Persons with drug addictions
- Immigrants
- Persons living in poverty
- Homeless persons
- Ages ranging from three-months to 70+ years old. This is not a typo. Instances of babies being sex trafficked as young as three months of age have been documented. In 2017, a three-month-old baby and her five-year-old sister were rescued during a sex trafficking FBI operation (Rosenberg, 2017).
- People from middle- and upper-class families
- College students
- People who are dressed nicely
- Introverted or extraverted people

The list could go on, but the point I hope is evident. Just as I previously noted about the characteristics of sex traffickers, anyone can be a victim of sex trafficking.

References

Burke, M.C. (2013). Human Trafficking. Routledge.

Rosenberg, E. (2017, October). Infant and her 5-year-old sister, allegedly on sale for $600, rescued in FBI sex trafficking sweep. The Washington Post, https://www.washingtonpost.com/news/true-crime/wp/2017/10/19/infant-and-young-child-among-the-more-than-80-victims-rescued-in-major-fbi-sex-trafficking-sweep/.

"The Realities of Sex Trafficking", by David W. Wahl, February 8, 2021.

Could it be that Christian anti-sex traffickers, like Caine, solicit large evangelical audiences and prop up a legal system that criminalizes sex work because they are better story tellers than their opponents?

Sex worker rights activists offer accounts of women, men and trans-people who migrate to new countries; who turn tricks on the street, acts as escorts, perform sex acts on camera, strip or whatever, to make ends meet; who fear police crackdowns and try to avoid deportation.

Christian anti-trafficking activists, instead, paint dramatic pictures of millions of innocent, vulnerable (even desirable?) victims: women and girls under threat of the voracious appetites of a cruel and dehumanizing sex trade, and they need you to rescue them.

VIEWPOINT

> "Not all sex workers come from marginalized social positions. As more people have been struggling before and during the pandemic to make ends meet, more people are becoming open to working in sex industries."

Sex Work Is a Choice, Not Exploitation

Angela Jones

In this viewpoint Angela Jones discusses changing attitudes toward sex work—especially online sex work—in recent years. She explains how the increase in sex work opportunities relates to the recent uptick in gig work and the internet as a tool for these workers. She challenges some stereotypes about sex work—such as that only desperate, marginalized people do it—by pointing out that many workers surveyed consider it preferable to other types of work available, and that some even consider it empowering. The flexibility and autonomy offered by online sex work makes it an appealing option for many people, especially those who would struggle to find more conventional work. Angela Jones is an associate professor of sociology at Farmingdale State College in Farmingdale, New York.

"Sex Work, Part of the Online Gig Economy, Is a Lifeline for Marginalized Workers," by Angela Jones, The Conversation, May 17, 2021, https://theconversation.com/sex-work-part-of-the-online-gig-economy-is-a-lifeline-for-marginalized-workers-160238. Licensed under CC BY-ND 4.0 International.

As you read, consider the following questions:
1. What impacts has the internet had on sex work?
2. According to Jones, how has the internet improved the lives of sex workers?
3. How did the 2018 federal law discussed in this viewpoint impact sex work?

More people are getting involved in more types of sex work, especially with the help of the internet, despite criminalization of their occupations and activist opposition, some of which threatens people's lives. My research interviewing a wide range of sex workers finds that more people are involved in the industry, including marginalized people who are finding it a literal lifeline in tough economic times.

The internet has diversified forms of sex work, aided in the industry's growth and interconnected previously unconnected types of sex work. Demand for amateur, non-studio-based porn has grown, expanding online pornographic industries like camming, in which performers interact with viewers. Online sex workers post content on specialized hosting sites. Other websites connect phone sex workers with new customers.

Some sites facilitate sugaring relationships, in which one person gives another money over time in exchange for a relationship lasting beyond a one-time encounter. On other sites, people can even sell used panties.

Especially during a global pandemic with more people out of work and searching for job opportunities, the modern sex industry is incorporating many new providers, customers and job possibilities.

Who Works in Modern Sex Industries?

Sex work has become more appealing to more laborers across social classes. In particular, online sex work has become more popular because it offers physical safety to those working fully online and minimizes risk to those laboring offline, has minimal requirements for employment and offers the potential for decent wages and autonomy.

These conditions create better work experiences. Sex worker Trip Richards said, "as a transgender man, . . . sharing my work on online platforms has offered me financial freedom and personal happiness I never thought possible and has allowed me to stay safe while pursuing my own goals as an artist, educator and activist."

Online sex work is a better option than the poorly remunerated work available to some people. Many sex workers, especially those from marginalized groups, have told me they found it difficult or impossible to get or keep jobs in other industries, making sex work their only option to earn a living. People with disabilities and chronic illnesses who participated in my research on the camming industry highlighted online sex work as flexible labor.

In my field, researchers assign first-name aliases to those we interview. One woman whom I call Kim remarked that camming is "easier to work with bipolar disorder." Amelia explained, "I have Crohn's and was unable to hold down a regular job. . . . My parents had no money, and I felt guilty asking them for help."

The sexual gig economy can be a refuge from the discrimination some people face in the nonsexual labor market. Natalie told me: "It's hard to find full-time work even at a fast food place as a full-time trans female who is pre-op and not on hormone replacement therapy."

Not all sex workers come from marginalized social positions. As more people have been struggling before and during the pandemic to make ends meet, more people are becoming open to working in sex industries.

What Do Sex Workers Earn?

In my study of the global camming industry, surveying and interviewing workers worldwide, full-time performers could earn US$10,000 a month. But those uncommonly high wages went almost exclusively to young, white, thin cisgender women. "Cisgender" is an adjective derived from the Latin prefix meaning "on the same side as" and refers to people who identify with the gender assigned to them at birth. In general, trans men are men who were assigned female at birth; trans women are women who were assigned male at birth.

Most of the top earners are from the U.S., and spent years building a brand. But most cam models work part-time, and median earnings were $1,000 a month overall, with trans women right at that average, but cisgender women $1,250 and cisgender men $350.

Online phone sex workers might charge $2 per minute, earning them $120 per hour, before the platform takes 30%. A model posting content on a subscription site might charge as much as $15 per month, though these sites generally take between 20%-30%.

Escorts, who provide companionship offline, often charge the highest rates of sex workers online. But their rates don't necessarily reflect their earnings. How much an escort might make depends on consumer demand and the number of clients they see each month.

Their schedules vary and they often do multiple types of sex work simultaneously. For example, Lenny told me, "I created an online persona, a profile for the purpose to offering escort services, selling homemade porn video clips, and an additional feature is webcamming, which I utilize by creating live sex shows to replicate what customers could experience during escort meetings face-to-face."

What Are the Benefits of Online Sex Work?

Like other gig workers, sex workers do not receive benefits such as employer-provided health care, vacation or retirement packages in many countries. And they have to do a lot of administrative work: marketing, messaging with clients, planning shoots or shows, preparing legal forms and dealing with constantly changing legal requirements and stringent websites' terms of service. However, sex workers describe other benefits.

Among workers in my camming study, 56.2% said they were not motivated to cam by money only. Carl told me, "The benefits of cam work are much the same as most independent jobs. You work at home on your own schedule and avoid the 9-to-5 daily grind." Workers like Halona said that being an independent entrepreneur provides autonomy and allows for creativity, describing online sex work as "the job I feel least exploited for my labor."

For some performers, this labor has allowed them to explore their sexuality, and as several said, they have "orgasms for a living." Others told me the work had helped boost their self-esteem, was affirming and brought them pleasure. As Whitney explained,

> I have a physical disability [spinal muscular atrophy] … and had recently moved … I wasn't working, and, honestly, I spent a lot of time at home bored and lonely. I started posting nudes on a social site and fell in love. I can remember being younger, watching porn, and thinking no one would want to see me doing that. With the support of my husband, I started camming. People did want to see me, and I really did love it.

How Has the Internet Changed Working Conditions?

The internet has helped improve sex workers' lives, including by keeping them safer. For those with internet access, escorts can screen clients online, making clients verify identity and provide references. Escorts develop and rely on online client review systems and community web forums, making them less dependent on exploitative third parties.

However, sex workers laboring offline and on the street remain at high risk. Continued criminalization of in-person sex work in the U.S. and other countries and governmental attempts at regulating sexual commerce online, limit consensual sex workers' opportunities.

In 2018, a federal law made internet platforms legally responsible if they hosted user-generated content related to sex work, which led free advertising platforms like Craigslist to shut down their personals sections. Other online review forums shut down. Those changes reduced the ability of internet services to keep sex workers safe—even in countries where consensual sex work is decriminalized.

VIEWPOINT 3

> "Whether or not you yourself can imagine wanting to be a sex worker, these voices should be allowed to speak for themselves. . . . How can I, therefore, assume to know the mind of every other woman? How can I assume to know what is better for another woman than she herself does?"

Sex Work Abolitionists Deny Sex Workers Agency

Victoria Bateman

In this excerpted viewpoint Victoria Bateman discusses how debates about abolishing sex work often revolve around bodily modesty. Society encourages girls and women to be modest, hide their bodies, and not engage in sexual behavior outside of the confines of marriage. Women who do not do so, the argument goes, present temptations for men, threatening both their own safety and the social order. Even radical feminists and secular abolitionists approach the issue in this way, arguing that it's for the benefit of women that sex work be eliminated while ignoring input from actual sex workers. In this way they deny sex workers the right to control what they do with their bodies, which denies them the right to engage in work they consider consensual and financially beneficial. Victoria Bateman

"How Decriminalisation Reduces Harm Within and Beyond Sex Work: Sex Work Abolitionism as the 'Cult of Female Modesty' in Feminist Form," by Victoria Bateman, *Sexuality Research and Social Policy*, July 15, 2021, https://link.springer.com/article/10.1007/s13178-021-00612-8. Licensed under CC BY.

Sexual Consent

is a British feminist economist and a fellow in economics at Cambridge University.

As you read, consider the following questions:

1. What does "the cult of female modesty" Bateman describes in this viewpoint involve?
2. Why do Bateman and other sources cited take issue with the idea of "buying women" put forth by radical feminists?
3. How does Bateman believe discussions of female modesty and sex work prioritize the male gaze instead of female experience? What is the problem with this?

Sex work has a long history and takes different forms, but the associated precarity and danger, particularly where poorer women and minorities are concerned, is undeniable. There is growing evidence that decriminalization reduces harm, and, indeed, it is the policy approach favored by sex worker groups. Despite this, many feminists instead seek to "end demand" for paid sex, recommending legal penalties for sex buyers, with the aim of abolishing sex work altogether.

[…]

Sex Work Abolitionism: the "Cult of Female Modesty" in Disguise

For centuries, women's bodies have been seen as sinful, and a woman's respect, worth and value rested delicately on her bodily modesty: on where a woman found herself on the continuum between "good girl" and "whore." Bodily modesty was deemed necessary both for individual women to protect themselves from harm—by keeping their "temptations" under wraps—and for wider social order. Immodest women were thought to provoke sin, leading to a breakdown of society. As such, they were singled out, punished and stigmatized. Patriarchy benefited: it was able to take what the "whores" had to offer while at the same time limiting their power, and it gave men a useful bargaining chip that could be used against all women, as we see in "Susanna and the Elders." As Karras (1996, p. 108) notes, for a long time, "[t]he arena of sexuality was the only one in which women could compete with men in importance . . . and it was the one in which men most feared they would not be able to control them." Associating women's bodies with sin and immorality was one way to take back control, while characterizing women as temptresses allowed men to behave in whatever way they liked, guilt-free. Men could abuse and mistreat women while taking the "moral high ground," pinning the punishment as deserved and in the best interest of wider society. Women's bodies were fair game.

When it comes to women themselves, it is difficult to see how they could ever "win" from this "cult of female modesty." As MacKinnon (1989, p. 110) herself notes, "Virtuous girls, virginal, are 'attractive,' up on those pedestals from which they must be brought down; unvirtuous girls, whores, are 'provocative,' so deserve whatever they get." The only way for women to earn popular respect was to abide by the modesty norms, which meant marking themselves out from other women; engaging in slut-shaming. This type of world is not one that has ever proved to be commensurate with gender equality. Indeed, where such modesty norms are most clearly practiced in the world today, one finds unequal opportunities and unequal rights for women. But, the "cult of female modesty" lives on in the Western World today, albeit holding women to a different "modesty" standard. Wendy Shalit's best-selling American book calls for *A Return to Modesty* (2014) and "Purity Culture" is popular within the growing Evangelical movement, something which has been linked to rape culture and abuse within these communities (Allison, 2021; Klement & Sagarin, 2017; Moon & Reger, 2014). Gabby Aossey writes that "[h]ip Feminist campaigns like Free the Nipple only encourage a gullible behavior of disrespect for our own bodies, leading to everyone else around us disrespecting our bodies as well . . . Muslim woman get respect and are looked at beyond aesthetics; they are actually taken seriously in their communities" (Aossey, 2017). But this renewed emphasis on female modesty is not only a feature of religious groups, it also manifests itself in feminist circles: in the lack of respect radical feminism offers to "immodest women," and most notably sex workers. As we will further see in what follows, this is visible, firstly, in the language employed within the abolitionist lobby, and, secondly, in the dismissal of sex workers' voices.

According to the artist Claire Bentley-Smith, described as "working closely" with the Leeds-based UK organization "Save Our Eyes," an organization which successfully challenged the street sex work managed zone, sex workers are "broken dolls" (Hyde, 2018). Bentley-Smith has therefore built sculptures made from rubbish, consisting of broken doll heads, monopoly money, drug refuse, or dirty bits of discarded underwear (Hyde, 2018). As Lister and Campbell (2018) responded: "They are not broken doll heads, monopoly money, drug refuse, or dirty bits of discarded underwear—the women working on the street in Leeds are human beings." As Gemma Ahearne has tweeted: "When I was a dancer aged 18–23, people spoke to me like rubbish. They spoke about dancers as . . . polluting. I vowed I would never let another dancer feel like that. The abolitionists are pushing 'purity culture.'" Just as Claire Bentley-Smith compares sex workers with "broken dolls" and rubbish, Natasha Walter refers to women more generally who could be thought of as immodest as "living dolls" (Walter, 2011). Carole Pateman claims that "[p]rostitution remains morally undesirable" (Pateman, 1983, p. 56); even though she characterizes sex workers as victims as opposed to immoral beings, the fact that she cannot find any value in or respect for the work sex workers perform (in fact, radical feminism will not even recognize sex work as work), speaks volumes. Without realizing it, one victim of sexual abuse in the workplace sums up the general disrespect which sex workers are afforded by society: "I felt like a prostitute, an utter disappointment to myself, my parents, my friends" (Berg, 2020, p.

272). As Zatz suggests, perhaps it is "not sex work per se" that is the problem but instead "the particular cultural and legal production of a marginalized, degraded prostitution that ensures its oppressive characteristics while acting to limit the subversive potential that might attend a decriminalized, culturally legitimized form of sex work" (Zatz, 1997, p. 291). Hence the call made by sex workers in the World Charter for Prostitutes' Rights "to change social attitudes which stigmatize and discriminate against prostitutes and ex-prostitutes of any race, gender or nationality" (see Weiss, 2018, p. 304).

Throughout radical feminist and abolitionist discussion of sex work one finds use of the phrase "buying women." For example, the 2008 report published by the Women's Support Project was titled "A Research Report Based on Interviews with 110 Men Who *Bought* Women in Prostitution" (Macleod et al., 2008; emphasis added). Julie Bindel (2020) writes of "punters, many of whom travel from outside of the city, are able to buy a woman with the same ease with which they might pick up a burger." Carole Pateman writes that "when a prostitute contracts out the use of her body she is . . . selling herself in a very real way" (Pateman, 1988, p. 207). Alison Jaggar writes that "since, unlike a man, she [a woman] is defined largely in sexual terms, when she sells her sexuality she sells herself" (Jaggar, 1991, p. 274).

But, as Zatz responds, when a female sex worker sells sex to a male client: "Possibly she is selling his image of her sexuality—but this image is not herself . . . There is no more reason to think that sex workers cannot separate their work from their sex life than there is to think that therapists cannot separate their work from their emotional life" (Zatz, 1997, p. 298). And, as *A Vindication of the Rights of Whores* makes clear, "feminists have to realize that all work involves selling some part of your body. You might sell your brain, you might sell your back, you might sell your fingers for typewriting. Whatever it is that you do you are selling one part of your body. I choose to sell my body the way I want to and I choose to sell my vagina" (Pheterson, 1989, p. 146). While radical feminists suggest that men see women as "sex objects," their own use of language suggests something similar when it comes to sex workers. The notion that buying *sex* is equivalent to buying a *woman*, seems to suggest that radical feminists themselves—somewhat ironically—see the women involved as just sex objects. Of course, by reducing a sex worker's identity down to one single identifying feature—sex—radical feminism is, conveniently, able to escape the uncomfortable comparison with care work altogether (Scoular, 2004, p. 345).

In addition to its use of language, a further way in which radical feminisms' disrespect for sex workers manifests itself is in its dismissal of sex workers' own voices. Let us first of all take a look at a couple of these voices.

In the words of the sex work activist Laura Lee (2014):

> I don't ask you to like what I do . . . what I do ask for is to be allowed to do my job in safety and to be treated with dignity and respect . . . there is no greater feeling than meeting a disabled person who has never been with a woman and affording them their first orgasm. To bring such happiness and fulfilment into someone's life is something I treasure. Sex work is work, just like any other. And those of us in the industry deserve support and respect—not to be reviled and stigmatized.

And, as Kirio Birks (2018), a defender of Grid Girls, notes:

> [S]urely a woman has a right to be the object of somebody else's desire if she wants and surely it doesn't matter if she is being paid for it? . . . Rather than sending Grid Girls off into the wilds of unemployment, or providing one less place for would-be models, a far better solution would have been to make sure that they're unionized, properly paid, and protected. If they are, then they have empowered other women to take up work they might otherwise have avoided, in a safer way.

Whether or not you yourself can imagine wanting to be a sex worker, these voices should be allowed to speak for themselves. Once, I could not imagine how any woman would want to pose or protest naked; now I do it myself. How can I, therefore, assume to know the mind of every other woman? How can I assume to know what is better for another woman than she herself does? How can I discount the voices of individual sex workers who demand rights and recognition, not "end demand"?

Here, however, radical feminists think they do have just cause to override sex workers' voices. Their first defence is that of "socialization," or what a Marxist would call "false consciousness." From Simone de Beauvoir (1949) to Natasha Walter (2011), feminist theorists have long argued that women are socially conditioned to behave in a way that benefits the patriarchy. For some abolitionists, this carries the implication that sex workers who speak out against the "end demand" approach can be conveniently ignored; they are presumed to be speaking on behalf of "pimps and punters" rather than for themselves. Hence, while prominent Labour Members of the UK Parliament, such as Sarah Champion and Jess Philipps, more normally emphasize the importance of listening to workers, they do not do so when it comes to sex workers, who are assumed to be victims rather than "workers."

But, isn't it intellectually elitist for radical feminists to assume that they know better than sex workers themselves? As Zatz notes, "attributions of false consciousness carry tremendous drawbacks. For starters, they are radically undemocratic, setting up a privileged group (usually intellectuals) to interpret the experience of others for them" (Zatz, 1997, p. 296). Isn't the whole point of feminism to listen to the voices of women, particularly those seen as at the margins of society? As one active member of #Labour4Decrim (a group tied to the UK Labour Party, supporting sex workers and allies), tweeted in December 2020, "I'm sick of women labour members and trade unionists slapping themselves on the back and saying that women need to be heard and then ignoring and talking over sex workers who are trying to do that." Ensuring that all women have voices and choices should be the feminist goal, and that goal can be achieved while welcoming sex workers, recognizing their voice and ensuring they have the same rights as any other worker. The policy package which sex workers themselves favor—a three-pronged approach of decriminalization, poverty-reduction and tackling borders—is one that can both reduce the number of non-consensual sex workers and also avoid hurting consensual sex workers. Once one entertains the possibility that sex work involves a whole range of experiences, and that these experiences are shaped by the law, by poverty and by stigma, it is a policy approach that, on a theoretical as well as practical level, trumps the blunter "end demand" approach.

Not only does radical feminism reduce sex workers' voices and demands down to the "pimp lobby," it, albeit subtly, prioritises male experiences ahead of female ones. Bindel (2017a, b) argues that many of the organizations supporting or campaigning for decriminalization are backed by the "pimp lobby," and so we can effectively ignore them. Despite the evidence Amnesty International received from numerous sex workers, the fact that a man who owns an escort business spoke in favor of decriminalization at one of their annual general meetings is, according to Bindel, reason to ignore Amnesty's extensive work showing that decriminalization is better for sex workers. She also noted that: "[a] legal challenge to the law in Northern Ireland is being led by Laura Lee, a 'sex workers' rights' campaigner—whose backers include the pimp Peter McCormick. I hope Lee loses" (Bindel, 2017a, b). Lee was a sex worker and sex work activist who wanted to reverse Northern Ireland's implementation of "end demand" because it made her feel less safe. But, because McCormick would benefit, this is thought to be enough to override Lee's own safety.

In regard to the impact of decriminalization in New Zealand, Bindel (2017a, b) writes that: "Views differ as to whether decriminalization has made the situation better or worse. One report, published five years after decriminalization, claimed it had little impact on the number of people working in the sex trade but had offered some safeguards to children and others. But the personal testimony of women who have been prostituted provides evidence that brothel owners and punters have benefited more than the women have." She nevertheless does not support New Zealand's decriminalization. Despite the fact that it has resulted in greater "safeguards," because brothel owners and punters have benefitted, it would have been better, apparently, if it hadn't happened.

So, should we more generally enact policy in a way that ensures that what are seen as male "aggressors" don't benefit, even if it comes at a cost to women? Male rapists might benefit from the fact that we live in a country where women are free to leave their homes unaccompanied, unlike in communities which practice purdah. Does that mean that women's freedom to roam should come second? That's what Bindel's approach to sex work would seem to suggest, though her well known objection to police advice for women to "stay indoors" when the Yorkshire Ripper was on the loose reveals a degree of inconsistency. Surely, the interests of men—even criminal men or men we might consider "immoral"—should not override the voices and interests of women? If sex workers prefer decriminalization, that should speak for itself.

In numerous ways, and across the world, the daily life of women is dictated by the way heterosexual men are assumed to "see;" by the "male gaze." It is the male way of viewing and experiencing the world that overrides what a woman herself would like to do and how she herself witnesses the world. If she wants to cool down, whether by removing her headscarf or her bikini top, that comes second to concerns about how a man might view her uncovered body. If she wants to show off her personality, rejecting conformity, that is, once again, overridden by how a man might interpret her state of dress. If she wants to protest naked, that must come second to how men might "benefit" from the sight of her body. As Emily Channell writes, "[m]ainstream women's organizations and many academic feminists see Femen's topless actions as simply giving men more of what they want—easily accessible women's bodies" (Channell, 2014, p. 613). On that basis, the tactics of not only Femen but also Pussy Riot, #freethenipple and my own activism are deemed "unfeminist" (Channell, 2014; Rivers, 2017; Matich et al., 2019). Hence why Tim Young of the Fox TV channel can tweet in response to my protests that "[t]here's nothing more antifeminist than having to strip naked desperate for a man's attention." The priority given to the male gaze means that a woman is judged on something other than her own terms, and is expected to dress and behave in a way that is dictated by how men might think and feel; if men might benefit from a particular action, then a woman should not do it—even if she wants to do it. Limiting men's "benefit" is more important than a woman acting in her own self interest.

Living our lives in a way that is *limited* by the male gaze as a means to *escape* the male gaze would seem to be a pyrrhic victory. The solution to women being viewed as "sex objects" is to be found in changing the way we as a society judge women, rather than in changing (and restricting) women's behavior. When I employ someone to move my heavy academic books, it is typically a man who arrives at my door, but that does not mean that I objectify men as existing to fulfill my muscle-based needs, seeing them a "cart horses." Where men choose to see women as sexual objects, it is they—and not women themselves—who are to blame. Just because some women do not cover their bodies is no excuse for people to think that women are "just bodies," and just because some women sell sex is no excuse for men thinking that women are simply "sexual objects" available for the taking. After all, I'm perfectly able to respect a man whatever he is or isn't wearing; it would, to my mind, be superficial to judge another person based on their state of dress. And I, for one, am also perfectly capable of respecting people who sell sex. Similarly, just because a woman makes you a coffee, or makes your hotel bed, does not mean that you should assume that all women exist to serve your basic needs. If men feel sexually entitled to women's bodies, and if women's respect and worth hangs on something as flimsy as a piece of cloth, we really do have a problem, but that problem is not uncovered women or sex workers: should women *really* have to cover up—or only have sex for free—in order to earn respect? The problem is in the collective beliefs of a society that judges women based on their bodily modesty, with those deemed "whores" expected to shoulder the blame for what happens in the heads of (some) men. As Priscilla Alexander has elsewhere pointed out, abolitionist feminists sexualizing the notion that the "whore" is "the cause of women's pain," and women will never be free until they are no longer afraid of this very word (Alexander, 1997, p. 83). What we find in radical feminism is the goal of completely abolishing sex work, the ultimate form of "whore-phobia."

Perhaps, however, this argument is best made by turning to sex workers' own voices. Let's begin with a letter which a sex worker sent to the American group Women Against Pornography, now housed in the Schlesinger Library archive at the Radcliffe Institute of Harvard University:

> "I recently heard one of your members say that porn films caused rape. I work in sex films. I don't think that women who appear sexy, either in film or in person are to blame for rape. The blame lies with the rapist—so let's not make excuses for his crime ... To say that looking at a sexy picture makes a normal, healthy man go out and rape is crazy. Most of the men I meet would not force themselves on me, and the ones who would, would do so even if they never saw an X rated film" (Exhibited at Museum of City of New York in 2018, courtesy of Schlesinger Library, Radcliffe Institute, Harvard University).

The same sex worker notes that she and her colleagues face violence of a sort ignored by the feminist group: violence from the authorities, which takes the form of "police violence every night." She adds that "you work hand in hand" with these authorities under the same banner of "cleaning up" the streets. The Yorkshire Ripper, who murdered numerous sex workers in the north of England in the 1970s and early 1980s, also claimed to be "cleaning up the streets" (Summers, 2008). As Roberts (1992) and Lowman (2000) have shown, "whore stigma" and the "discourse of disposal" fuels the violent treatment and murder of sex workers. Kinnell (2008) documents the way in which sex workers are portrayed as "social pollutants" and equated with rubbish. As Cunningham and Sanders (2017) conclude: "Only with a combination of anti-stigma work alongside meaningful legal and policy change that prioritizes sex worker safety can there be any hope of addressing the tragedy of sex worker homicide." As Laverte (2017) writes:

> There is a lack of understanding that first and foremost, it is social prejudices about prostitution that render it difficult for us to protect ourselves. That is because they lower the threshold to use violence against us—among clients, among the police, among everyone.

This same stigma affects the ability of law enforcement to catch those who are engaging in exploitation within the sex sector. The fear of being "outed" is a common fear, as a result of which many cases of abuse and exploitation go unreported (Payne, 2014). As Belinda Brooks-Gordon (2016) writes:

> [E]xploiters can only be held to account with an increased chance of being caught. Currently, the likelihood of being caught is low because sex workers are so stigmatized they are reluctant to report offenses. Decriminalization is an effective way to ensure that exploiters are more likely to be held to account (Barnet, 2004), as is making violence against sex workers a hate crime.

As Julia Laite notes of the "end demand" approach, it is "an ideal way to appear to crack down on prostitution without appearing to crack down on the women involved." In reality, "[t]he legal stigma of selling sex might be removed by a law that criminalizes clients and only clients, but the social stigma of engaging in the sex industry—even if it is claimed to be a choice made by an adult woman—still remains" and, as such, "end demand" still "maintains the age-old position that prostitution is inherently morally wrong" (Laite in McCarthy et al., 2015).

The "cult of female modesty" does not serve women well, whether sex workers or not. Not only does violence towards sex workers go unreported because of stigma and associated reputational fears, so too does abuse of nonsex workers in communities where the modesty cult is particularly strong. Zakaria et al. (2020) note that "[s]exual violence often goes unreported in

Pakistan, as victims risk being cast out by their parents, are forced to marry their rapists or are killed over the perceived injury to their families' honor." In recent years, stories of rape and murder of women in India and Pakistan have proliferated. On 1 December 2019 a female student in Pakistan was forcibly taken from her car by a group of five men. Here were just some of the responses (Chaturvedi & Niaz, 2019):

> "Jab mithayi ko khula chorro ge to makhyan zaroor ayen gi" (If you leave the sweet box open, it will inevitably attract flies).
>
> "Ye to hona hi tha, kapre to dekho" (This was inevitable, look at what she is wearing).
>
> "Well done kidnappers . . . Jo log apni bachio ko be lagaam chor dete hain. They deserve this" (Those who leave their daughters unconstrained deserve this).

This suggests that the problem is not "immodest" women but those who deem women to be unworthy based on what they judge to be "immodest" behavior; those who, as a result, see women as ripe for attack and punishment. Closer to home, and as Allison (2021) shows in her book #ChurchToo, the "purity culture" that exists within Evangelical Christianity "upholds abuse" within American communities.

So, in sum, are sex workers, pornography and scantily clad women (including myself) really what causes harm to womankind? Is abolishing pornography and "prostitution" really the best approach for tackling gender inequality? If "immodest" women and sexualized images of women were central to gender inequality, why are countries like Iran and Pakistan not at the top of the gender equality rankings? Perhaps it is because what causes most damage to womankind is not women who wander around scantily clad or who sell sex, but, instead, what happens in people's minds: the social belief that a woman's value rests on her physical modesty. It is *this* belief that not only causes harm to sex workers—causing clients to mistreat them and limiting their options to speak out for fear of their reputation—but that leads to men's guilt-free mistreatment of women who they more generally judge to be "trashy." In response to one of my naked protests, Deborah Kurbjuweit, who graduated from Berkeley, tweeted that I was fat and needed to lose weight, and then followed up with: "The body is sacred until you decide to give it over to gawking, opinionated onlookers. Then you get what you deserve." This attitude—one in which immodest women are fair game who "get what they deserve" is the ultimate problem, and it is a problem rooted in minds, not in immodesty. It is this same modesty cult that results in so many of the policies and practices that hurt women across the world. Those policies include controlling women's travel, where they work, and their clothing, all to supposedly "protect" them from mistreatment. It also includes social practices that involve cutting off women's genitals, compulsory virginity testing and "honor killings." Radical feminism should be challenging the modesty cult, not contributing to it with its insistence that sex workers are not welcome in the feminist utopia.

On one level, feminism of course rejects the idea that a woman's worth hangs on her body. But, at the same time, it nevertheless judges women based on what they do with that body, seeing gender inequality as the result of using that body in "immodest" ways. Of course, so as not to appear as if one is blaming women themselves for the resultant gender inequality, immodest women have to be cast as unwilling victims. It is simply inconceivable that any woman would choose to be a sex worker if you believe that a woman's value rests on her bodily modesty; but, once we escape from the "cult of female modesty," sex workers voices start to make sense, and the idea of "abolishing" them is revealed for what it is. That is, a morally driven and intellectually elitist project in which a group of "clever" women are ganging up to deny women on the margins of society the rights and freedoms that they themselves benefit from. It is a battle in which women who monetize their brains are denying others the freedom to monetize their bodies.

For centuries, men have regulated and restricted what women can do with their bodies and with their brains. Over the last century, women have taken great strides in terms of their ability to use their brains as they wish. However, the same cannot be said of their bodies. Show too much of that body, and you'll be accused—as I so often am accused—of objectifying and sexualizing yourself, of "setting feminism back a hundred years" and of "embarrassing" womankind. And, whilst freely making money from your brain is to be celebrated, making money from your body is, apparently, not. Ultimately, isn't it inconsistent to allow women to both uncover and make money from their brains but not to uncover or make money from their bodies? A good chunk of modern day—radical—feminism looks increasingly hypocritical, intellectually elitist and unfair. It has far too many overlaps with historic moralistic-driven campaigns to abolish sex work, and with those who persist in the modern day with blaming society's problems on the immodest behavior of women.

[…]

References

Alexander, P. (1997). Feminism, sex workers, and human rights. In J. Nagle (Ed.), *Whores and Other Feminists* (pp. 83–97). Routledge.

Allison, E. J. (2021). *#ChurchToo: How purity culture upholds abuse and how to find healing*. Broadleaf Books.

Aossey, G. (2017). *Muslims are the true feminists*. Huffington Post.

Berg, H. (2020). Left of #MeToo. *Feminist Studies, 46*(2), 259–286.

Bindel, J. (2020). *How Leeds enables 'paid rape'*. UnHerd.

Bindel, J. (2017a). *Why Prostitution should never be legalised*. The Guardian.

Bindel, J. (2017b). *The pimping of prostitution: Abolishing the sex work myth*. Palgrave Macmillan.

Birks, K. (2018). *Grid girls and puritans*. Quillette.

Brooks-Gordon, B. (2016). Written evidence submitted by Dr Belinda Brooks-Gordon to the Home Affairs Committee. http://data.parliament.uk/writtenevidence/committeeevidence.svc/evidencedocument/home-affairs-committee/prostitution/written/29130.pdf

Channell, E. (2014). Is sextremism the new feminism? Perspectives from Pussy Riot and Femen. *Nationalities Papers, 42*(4), 611–614.

Chaturvedi, A., & Niaz, L. (2019). *Parallels in gender violence in India and Pakistan*. South Asia LSE Blog.

Coalition Against Trafficking in Women. (2005). Survivors of prostitution and trafficking manifesto: who represents women in Prostitution?

Cunningham, S., & Sanders, T. (2017). *Sex work and homicide*. University of Leicester Briefing Paper.

de Beauvoir, S. (1949). *The second sex*. Penguin.

Dworkin, A. (1993). Prostitution and male supremacy. *Michigan Journal of Gender and Law, 1*(1), 1–12.

Hyde, N. (2018). *Why a Leeds woman is making sculptures out of prostitutes' rubbish*. Leeds Live.

Jaggar, A. (1991). Prostitution. In A. Soble (Ed.), T*he philosophy of sex: Contemporary readings*. London: Rowan and Littlefield.

Karras, R. M. (1996). *Common women: Prostitution and sexuality in medieval England*. Oxford University Press.

Kinnell, H. (2008). *Violence and sex work in Britain*. Willan Publishing.

Klement, K. R., & Sagarin, B. J. (2017). Nobody wants to date a whore: Rape-supportive messages in women-directed Christian dating books. *Sexuality & Culture, 21*, 205–223.

Laverte, M. (2017). *Sexual violence and prostitution: The problem is your image of us*. Die Tageszeitung.

Lee, L. (2014). Sex workers want rights - Not rescue. Ravishly.

Lister, K., & Campbell, R. (2018). Rubbishing sex workers: the danger of discarding sex worker safety. Whores of Yore Blog. https://www.thewhoresofyore.com/sex-worker-voices/rubbishing-sex-workers-the-danger-of-discarding-sex-worker-safety

Lowman, J. (2000). Violence and the outlaw status of (street) prostitution in Canada. *Violence against Women, 6*(9), 987–1011.

MacKinnon, C. (1989). *Toward a feminist theory of the state*. Harvard University Press.

Macleod, J., Farley, M., Anderson, L., & Golding, J. (2008). A research report based on interviews with 110 men who bought women in prostitution. Women's Support Project.

Matich, M., Ashman, R., & Parsons, E. (2019). #freethenipple – Digital activism and embodiment in the contemporary feminist movement. *Consumption Markets & Culture,22*(4), 337–362.

McCarthy, H., Caslin, S., Laite, J. (2015). *Prostitution and the law in historical perspective: a dialogue*. History & Policy.

Moon, S., & Reger, J. (2014). "'You are not your own'": Rape, sexual assault, and consent in Evangelical Christian dating books. *Journal of Integrated Social Sciences, 4*, 55–74.

Pateman, C. (1983). Defending prostitution: Charges Against Ericsson. *Ethics, 93*.

Pateman, C. (1988). *The sexual contract*. Polity Press.

Payne, T. (2014). *Escort worker plunged 100ft to her death off hotel balcony after client told parents about her secret life*. Manchester Evening News.

Pheterson, G. (Ed.). (1989). *A vindication of the rights of whores: The international movement for prostitutes' rights*. Seattle: Seal.

Rivers, N. (2017). Femen: Postfeminist playfulness or reinforcing sexualized stereotypes? In N. Rivers (Ed.), *Postfeminism(s) and the arrival of the fourth wave* (pp. 79–105). Palgrave Macmillan.

Roberts, N. (1992). *Whores in history: Prostitution in Western Society*. Grafton.

Scoular, J. (2004). The 'subject' of prostitution. *Feminist Theory, 5*(3), 343–355.

Summers, C. (2008). *'Easy targets' for predators*. BBC News.

Walter, N. (2011). *Living Dolls*. Frankfurt: Fischer-Taschenbuch

Weiss, P. A. (2018). *Feminist manifestos: A global documentary reader*. New York University Press.

Zakaria, A. Mughal, J., & Abi-Habib, M. (2020). *Women face dilemma in a war zone: Risk the blasts or sexual assault*. New York Times.

Zatz, N. D. (1997). Sex work/sex act: Law, labour, and desire in constructions of prostitution. *Signs, 22*(2), 277–308.

VIEWPOINT 4

> "Rather than making the value judgment that sexual labor is immoral, and should therefore be criminal, policymakers should adopt a labor and human rights perspective that affirms the autonomy and dignity of people engaged in sexual labor."

There Are Ways to End Violence Against Sex Workers

Jayne Swift

In the following viewpoint Jayne Swift argues that it makes sense to decriminalize sex work. She explains that keeping sex work criminalized puts sex workers at risk of physical and sexual violence, since they feel they cannot count on the police and criminal justice system to protect them, and clients who become violent know it is unlikely they will get the police involved. Swift then outlines ways to accomplish decriminalization at the local, state, and federal level. Jayne Swift is a managing editor of the Gender Policy Report *and an independent scholar.*

This article was originally published by the Gender Policy Report, a project by the Center on Women, Gender, and Public Policy at the Humphrey School of Public Affairs, University of Minnesota. Jayne Swift, "How to End Violence Against Sex Workers," Gender Policy Report, December 14, 2022. https://genderpolicyreport.umn.edu/how-to-end-violence-against-sex-workers/

As you read, consider the following questions:

1. What are two outcomes of sex work criminalization, according to this viewpoint?
2. According to the author, do voters support decriminalization of sex work?
3. What are two steps that can help decriminalize sex work, as stated by Swift?

Imagine what it's like to work a job that is prohibited by local, state, and federal laws and policies. These policies make it extremely difficult to speak openly about or advertise your services, to secure safe, reliable spaces where you can work alone or with others, to utilize financial institutions, and to record your employment on official forms that may require it. You're constantly aware that your trade leaves you vulnerable to surveillance, arrest, and criminal prosecution.

This is the daily reality of sex workers. Criminalization leaves sex workers vulnerable to physical and sexual violence by those who understand the law to be on their side. Criminalization perpetuates structural violence against people in the sex trades, leading to housing precarity, poor health outcomes, exclusion from educational and employment opportunities, and incarceration.

Advocates will soon mark the International Day to End Violence Against Sex Workers, and it is past time for policymakers to decriminalize sex work.

Violence Against Sex Workers

Research shows that sex workers are particularly vulnerable to physical and sexual violence at work. Globally, sex workers have a 45–75% chance of experiencing sexual violence on the job. Individual studies of sex work in the U.S. confirm high rates of violence, often from law enforcement. Street workers (who are more likely to be of color, trans, and housing precarious), are especially vulnerable. One New York City-based study of street workers found that 80% had experienced violence and 30% reported violence or threats of violence from law enforcement. A similar study of indoor workers found that 46% had been victims of violence and 14% had experienced police violence. Migrants and LGBTQ sex workers are also more likely to encounter violence.

Criminalization Perpetuates Violence

Violence against sex workers is not inherent to the work but is exacerbated by criminalization. Sex work is criminalized through a mix of municipal, county, state, and federal laws, policies, and policing practices. Most prohibitions against commercial sex are laws that criminalize the activities surrounding commercial sex, including: advertising or soliciting for the purposes of prostitution, transporting people involved in sex work, renting property to or keeping a "house of prostitution," loitering, and assisting people involved in the sale of sexual services.

While no federal laws explicitly criminalize the sale of sex, federal policy has long adopted a hard line against sexual commerce through various immigration, interstate commerce, and anti-trafficking legislation. Sex trafficking is overwhelmingly conceptualized as a problem of crime control. Enormous resources have been allocated to law enforcement agencies and non-profit organizations that may offer very little in the way of social services. The crime control agenda leads to traumatizing raid and rescue operations, surveillance of internet platforms, and court-mandated "rehabilitation" programs. As many scholars have argued, anti-trafficking policies such as the Trafficking Protection Victims Act (2000) have reinforced punitive immigration policies that seek to deter migration.

Anti-trafficking policy—in both design and implementation— has been guided by harmful assumptions. These include a tendency to over-emphasize sex trafficking over far more common forms of labor trafficking, a deliberate conflation of trafficking and sex work, and the goal of abolishing commercial sex itself.

As a result, all people in the sex trades are impacted by anti-sex trafficking policy. These policies also do little to change the socioeconomic conditions that lead to trafficking or exploitation, particularly for those crossing borders. Instead, they have perpetuated further violence by expanding the law enforcement dragnet over people in the sex trades. The new "war on trafficking" harms the marginalized populations they claim to be rescuing.

Decriminalization Reduces Violence

Instead of trying to prohibit commercial sex, policy should seek to maximize the well-being of people engaged in it. Decriminalization is supported by leading civil rights, public health, human rights, and anti-trafficking organizations. Decriminalization means the repeal of all laws that criminalize the sale of sex amongst consenting adults, including laws that penalize clients or operating a brothel. Regulatory aspects, such as occupational health and safety standards for businesses, would be moved to the civil code.

New Zealand offers an example of decriminalization in practice. The Prostitution Reform Act (2003) decriminalized sex work, established health and safety regulations, and drew parameters around brothel operations. Trafficking and sex with minors remain a crime. Since its passage, violence and discrimination against sex workers has diminished; relations between sex workers, law enforcement, and civil society have improved; and rates of trafficking have not increased.

Racial justice advocates have long challenged the ever-expanding role that policing and prisons play in our society. Decriminalization of sex work is a concrete step that policymakers could take to weaken law enforcement power over and decrease violence against marginalized communities.

There is growing public support for decriminalization: recent polling found that a majority of voters support decriminalizing sex work, including 2/3 of voters age 18-44.

Path to Decriminalization:
Multiple steps can be taken on local, state, and federal levels to protect sex workers.

Local
Repeal local anti-loitering for the purposes of prostitution ordinances. These laws lead to arbitrary and discriminatory policing practices that do harm to cis and trans women of color.

State
- Advocate for safe reporting laws which allow sex workers to report violence or crimes committed against them without fearing arrest or prosecution
- Prohibit entrapment by state agents. It is not uncommon for law enforcement to entrap and engage in sexual conduct with sex workers in order to make prostitution arrests.
- Audit and end prostitution diversion programs. Researchers have found that these programs fail to achieve their goals and exercise coercive control over individuals.
- Pass policies that automatically expunge the criminal records of those with prostitution-related convictions. Without expungement, finding non-sex work employment and housing can be challenging.

Federal
- Support the Safe Sex Workers Study Act, which will initiate a federal study of the impact of the Fight Online Sex Trafficking Act. FOSTA has had a devastating impact on people in the sex trades and been found to be ineffective in a recent U.S. General Accounting Office review.
- Oppose the EARN-IT Act. This Act is touted as another anti-exploitation bill but is a cyber-surveillance measure. The EARN-IT Act would create a 19-person commission, headed by the U.S. Attorney General, empowered to create online

speech rules. The Act will likely lead to the deplatforming of and greater harm to sex workers.
- Repeal federal immigration policies that restrict the entry of anyone who has engaged in prostitution
- Demand that subsequent reauthorizations of PEPFAR, the major source of global funding for HIV/AIDS programs, repeal the anti-prostitution pledge which requires any organization receiving funding to state their opposition to "prostitution and sex trafficking."

How long must sex workers wait to be free from violence and harm?

The answer to this question is in many respects a matter of political will. Rather than making the value judgment that sexual labor is immoral, and should therefore be criminal, policymakers should adopt a labor and human rights perspective that affirms the autonomy and dignity of people engaged in sexual labor. The public has an important role to play in this fight, by advocating for pro-sex worker policies as part of a commitment to gender, racial, LGBTQ, and economic justice.

VIEWPOINT 5

> "Those who favour decriminalisation say it removes the stigma of prostitution and makes it easier for sex workers to go to the police if they need protection from violence."

Does It Make Sense to Decriminalize Sex Work?

Naomi Grimley

In the following viewpoint Naomi Grimley examines the debate around the issue of decriminalizing sex work. Grimley presents evidence from both sides of the debate. In support of decriminalization, she points out that it can help encourage sex workers to turn to law enforcement for protection and empower them to more openly negotiate safe sex practices with clients. However, others worry that decriminalizing the sex trade will lead to more human trafficking, as some studies suggest this correlation exists. She examines the evidence from two large country-level examples: the Nordic Model and the German experiment. Naomi Grimley is the global affairs correspondent for the BBC.

As you read, consider the following questions:

1. Why does Amnesty International favor decriminalization of sex work, according to this viewpoint?

"Amnesty International row: Should prostitution be decriminalised?," by Naomi Grimley, BBC, August 11, 2015. Reprinted with permission.

2. What did Germany hope would happen with decriminalization, according to the author?
3. Do lawmakers in the UK favor the Nordic Model?

It's not often that a liberal newspaper like *The Guardian* rails against an organization like Amnesty International.

But last week the paper ran a stinging editorial questioning the wisdom of the human rights group.

It said Amnesty would make a "serious mistake" if it advocated the decriminalisation of prostitution—a decision the group's international council will vote on later on Tuesday.

It's not just *The Guardian* that is upset. Several women's groups have got together with a host of big-name actresses—including Meryl Streep, Emma Thompson and Kate Winslet—to criticize Amnesty after a draft of its policy proposal was leaked.

Former U.S. President Jimmy Carter has also urged Amnesty to be very careful before it changes its stance.

The Arguments for Decriminalisation

Amnesty's leaked proposal says decriminalization would be "based on the human rights principle that consensual sexual conduct between adults is entitled to protection from state interference" so long as violence or child abuse or other illegal behavior isn't involved.

Those who favor decriminalization say it removes the stigma of prostitution and makes it easier for sex workers to go to the police if they need protection from violence.

It's also argued that it empowers prostitutes to strike open deals with their clients about safe sex. There are various groups across the world that support decriminalization, such as Durbar in India.

Germany is one of the countries which liberalized its prostitution laws, together with New Zealand and the Netherlands.

One of the main reasons the Germans opted for legalization in 2002 was the hope that it would professionalize the industry, giving prostitutes more access to benefits such as health insurance and pensions—just like in any other job.

Felcitas Schirow, a German brothel owner and sex worker, says the 2002 law has helped give prostitutes self-confidence.

"The owners of brothels could invest money," she says, "and the women could pick a good employer where they felt at home and who met their requirements."

Criticisms

But there are many who argue that the German experiment has gone badly wrong with very few prostitutes registering and being able to claim benefits. Above all, the number one criticism is that it's boosted sex tourism and fuelled human trafficking to meet the demand of an expanded market.

Figures on human trafficking and its relationship to prostitution are hard to establish. But one academic study looking at 150 countries argued there was a link between relaxed prostitution laws and increased trafficking rates.

Other critics of the German model point to anecdotal evidence of growing numbers of young Romanian and Bulgarian women travelling to Germany to work on the streets or even in mega-brothels.

An investigation in 2013 by *Der Spiegel* described how many of these women head to cities such as Cologne voluntarily but soon end up caught in a dangerous web they can't easily escape.

The Coalition Against Trafficking In Women argues that pimps would be the only ones to benefit from decriminalizing prostitution.

The Nordic Model

The women's groups and anti-trafficking campaigners opposing the Amnesty motion start from the premise that most prostitutes are victims who sell sex simply to survive.

They argue that human trafficking and prostitution are inextricably linked.

They think the best approach to prostitution is the "Nordic model". This is where the police go after the purchasers of sex by handing out tough fines or prison sentences to punters, and leave the sex workers in peace. In other words, the aim is to stifle demand.

It was a policy adopted by Sweden in 1999 and it's since been copied by a host of other countries including Iceland, Canada, Norway and most recently Northern Ireland.

The European Parliament wants more member countries to adopt the model.

Some MPs at Westminster also believe it should replace the confusing patchwork of laws in England and Wales (in summary: buying and selling sex isn't illegal but brothel-keeping, kerb-crawling and soliciting sex in a public place are).

What Does the Law Say About Paying for Sex in the UK?

- Often referred to as kerb crawling, it is illegal to approach someone in a public place to ask for their services as a prostitute.
- It is also illegal to persistently approach people in a public place to offer to sell them sexual services.
- But you are allowed to pay for sex if the person is over 18 and hasn't been forced into prostitution, apart from in Northern Ireland.
- Renting or allowing the use of your property as a brothel is forbidden.

But there are critics of the Nordic model too. Dr Jay Levy has studied the Swedish example and he's not convinced by police figures suggesting prostitution is in decline there.

Instead, he thinks the Swedes have just succeeded in pushing prostitution into more clandestine spaces, making it even more risky.

"It basically reduces safety," he says. "It reduces the amount of time that sex workers have to suss out a situation. And because clients are criminalized, they are reluctant to leave any information by which they can be traced."

Those pushing for decriminalization inside Amnesty International and their newfound opponents both say they want to protect the human rights of prostitutes.

But there's no getting around it—they each have very different approaches about how that's best achieved.

And they can't both be right.

Sexual Consent

Periodical and Internet Sources Bibliography

The following articles have been selected to supplement the diverse views presented in this chapter.

Nina Avramova, "More Violence, Sexual Infections When Sex Work Is Criminalized, Study Finds," CNN, December 11, 2018. https://www.cnn.com/2018/12/11/health/criminalizing-sex-work-more-violence-stds-intl/index.html.

Umberto Bacchi, "Legalizing Prostitution Lowers Violence and Disease," Reuters, December 11, 2018. https://www.reuters.com/article/idUSKBN1OA28M/.

Zach Budryk, "Poll: Majority Supports Decriminalizing Sex Work," the *Hill*, January 30, 2020. https://thehill.com/regulation/other/480725-poll-majority-supports-decriminalizing-sex-work/.

Kathleen Creedon, "A Job is a Job—Trafficking Laws Increase Stigma for Consensual Sex Workers," Texas Public Radio, April 22, 2022. https://www.tpr.org/government-politics/2022-04-22/a-job-is-a-job-trafficking-laws-increase-stigma-for-consensual-sex-workers.

Mackenzie Darling, "My Body, My Choice: Why the Decriminalization of Sex Work is Essential for Reproductive Justice," Georgetown Law, December 15, 2022. https://oneill.law.georgetown.edu/my-body-my-choice-why-the-decriminalization-of-sex-work-is-essential-for-reproductive-justice/.

Kate Fistric, "Violence Against Sex Workers Can Be Curbed—But Not with Our Current Policies," Volt, December 15, 2023. https://volteuropa.org/news/violence-against-sex-workers-can-be-curbed-but-not-with-our-current-policies.

Jasmine Garsd, "Should Sex Work be Decriminalized? Some Activists Say It's Time," NPR, March 22, 2019. https://www.npr.org/2019/03/22/705354179/should-sex-work-be-decriminalized-some-activists-say-its-time.

Dana Levy, "Can the Preconditions for True Consent Ever Exist in Prostitution?" Nordic Model Now, December 21, 2018. https://nordicmodelnow.org/2018/12/21/can-the-preconditions-for-true-consent-ever-exist-in-prostitution/.

Susan Nembhard, "Partial Decriminalization of Sex Work Could Cause More Harm Than Good," Urban Institute, April 15, 2021. https://www.urban.org/urban-wire/partial-decriminalization-sex-work-could-cause-more-harm-good.

Katie Smith, "Protecting Sex Workers: Why Are They Prone to Violence?" NewsNation, July 28, 2023. https://www.newsnationnow.com/crime/protecting-sex-workers-vulnerable-violence/.

Paige Sutherland, "Why Some Advocates are Pushing Back Against Decriminalization in the Sex Trade," WBUR, April 29, 2023. https://www.wbur.org/onpoint/2023/08/29/why-some-sex-workers-are-pushing-back-against-decriminalization-efforts.

CHAPTER 4

How Will the Topic of Sexual Consent Continue to Evolve?

Chapter Preface

The viewpoints in this chapter explore a wide range of topics related to what discussions around sexual consent could look like in the future and how to create a stronger culture of consent moving forward. Some viewpoints provide insight into the teaching of sexual consent, how it should be done, and whether simply teaching sexual consent is enough. They also consider the active role young people are taking in improving education about consent.

Other viewpoints look at the role that social movements, religious institutions, and those in power—especially men—play in this complex issue. How can there be any sexual consent when rich, powerful individuals demand sex from those who will suffer consequences if they don't obey? Do powerful institutions like the Catholic Church have a responsibility to punish offending clergy? And while as previous viewpoints have stated the #MeToo movement played an important role in starting conversations about consent, some question whether the movement has gone too far and added to the confusion around this issue and lead to the persecution of individuals who have not violated sexual consent.

Readers of these viewpoints will gain a stronger understanding of the current state of the sexual consent conversation, recent efforts to address the issue, and suggestions for what will and will not work to support sexual consent in the future.

VIEWPOINT 1

> "There are a lot of women who say it doesn't matter. If a few men get hurt in this reckoning, that's OK. And there are other people who say, you don't solve injustice with further injustice."

Has the #MeToo Movement Gone Off Track?
Michel Martin

In the following viewpoint Michel Martin conducts an interview with journalists Caitlin Flanagan and Anna North about the #MeToo movement. The writers dissect the movement and wonder if it has lost its original intentions. They claim that the #MeToo movement has led to a rise in false or overblown complaints against men in power, and that these accusations have the potential to cause harm. However, they also acknowledge that #MeToo has had the positive impact of allowing women to speak out about things that make them uncomfortable in sexual situations. Michel Martin is a journalist and correspondent for National Public Radio and WNET.

As you read, consider the following questions:

1. According to this viewpoint are there some men getting accused unjustly because of the #MeToo movement?

©2019 National Public Radio, Inc. NPR news report titled "Perspectives on the 'MeToo' Movement" by Michel Martin was originally published on September 1, 2019, and is used with the permission of NPR. Any unauthorized duplication is strictly prohibited.

2. According to North, what does it mean to "believe women" in this context?
3. According to Flanagan, how do false or overblown accusations harm other women?

Almost two years into the "Me Too" movement, NPR's Michel Martin talks about what justice in these cases should look like with Caitlin Flanagan of *The Atlantic* and *Vox*'s Anna North.

MICHEL MARTIN, HOST: These are tumultuous and intense days in the #MeToo movement, the global grassroots effort to address sexual misconduct by powerful men. This summer, *The New Yorker* raised questions about the complaints that caused former Minnesota Senator Al Franken to resign, suggesting some elements of the complaints were false or overblown, and there had been a rush to judgment. Last week, writer Emily Yoffe wrote a lengthy piece for *Reason* magazine raising questions about accusations that cost a former *Los Angeles Times* correspondent his job, noting that the reporter, Jonathan Kaiman, was struggling with thoughts of suicide. Her piece prompted several angry responses from other journalists accusing Yoffe of shaming and undermining women.

It's in that context that we wanted to talk about some of the issues that are emerging in this increasingly passionate debate about whether the #MeToo movement has gotten off track or perhaps not gone far enough, so we've called two writers who've taken this on. Caitlin Flanagan wrote for *The Atlantic* about the comic Aziz Ansari.

Caitlin, thank you for joining us.

CAITLIN FLANAGAN: Thanks for having me.

MARTIN: Anna North is a writer for *Vox* who critiqued Flanagan's piece among others, and I thank you so much for joining us once again.

ANNA NORTH: Thanks for having me.

MARTIN: Caitlin, I'm going to start with you because you wrote a piece last year entitled "The Humiliation Of Aziz Ansari." And it kind of described a lengthy piece that had been posted that described an encounter that a young woman had with Aziz Ansari. And you've written about #MeToo since then. What concerns you about what you're seeing?

FLANAGAN: Well, the #MeToo movement—you know, it came at us from zero to 100, which is often the way that powerful social movements operate. You know, there's oppression that lasts and lasts and lasts, and traditional techniques to overcome it don't work. And then suddenly, there'll be one thing that happens that—you know, in this case, the Harvey Weinstein case—where there's just this explosion. We can't take it anymore, and we're going to fix this problem by any means necessary.

So, on the one hand, I was astounded by how many really terrible things men whom I've had professional dealings with as a journalist were credibly accused of and lost their jobs over. And at the same time, you could see standing to the side that there was a lot of collateral damage that was going on and that when things slowed down, there'd be a reckoning. You know, if #MeToo was a reckoning, this moment as well is a reckoning.

There are a lot of women who say it doesn't matter. If a few men get hurt in this reckoning, that's OK. And there are other people who say, you don't solve injustice with further injustice. And in that case of Aziz Ansari, I thought that was a really scurrilous thing that that website did to post that piece about him.

MARTIN: And just—as briefly as you can, because you wrote a lengthy piece about it—what exactly did you consider scurrilous about it?

How Will the Topic of Sexual Consent Continue to Evolve?

FLANAGAN: Well, there was a young woman who had met him, and they went out to dinner, and they had a sexual encounter. And at one point, she said, I don't feel comfortable. And by her own very self-serving account, he immediately said, I never want you to feel uncomfortable. Let's put our clothes on. And to me, that's the sexual revolution. That's what a lot of women worked hard to gain for young women—the right to do that.

And if just the fact of saying I don't feel comfortable—if she wants something even more than that to be sort of perceived or mind-read by a sexual partner, I thought that was opportunistic. I thought it was vengeful. And I thought that what was really going on is that she wanted something from him that had to do with a very different thing from being sexual partners. She wanted affection. She wanted to matter. And that's not necessarily part of a casual sexual encounter. So I thought there was a bit of a grift that was beginning to work its way into the movement. And I thought we're all going to end up having to account for this. And ultimately, it's going to undermine the movement.

MARTIN: OK.

FLANAGAN: And I think, to a significant extent, it has.

MARTIN: Anna North, let's go to you now because the title of your piece for *Vox* says a lot, too. Your piece says, #MeToo's latest critics say they want to help the movement. Why are they shaming women? What's your take on the criticism of the movement, and what concerns you about that?

NORTH: I think that at this point in #MeToo - you know, we're two years into the sort of latest, most public phase - you know, it's been, as Caitlin said, you know, these two years of many very public allegations. And I do think it's a really great time to think about what consequences are appropriate, how do we do investigations correctly? I do think it's a great time to think about what justice looks like and how to really serve that for all parties involved in these kinds of things.

But the concern I have is that a lot of the conversations that I've seen around what does justice look like seem to sort of treat it as a zero-sum game where if we say we're concerned about maybe someone faced consequences that were too severe, maybe we don't like the way the investigation went, then it seems to go so quickly to shaming the women who came forward. So women who had allegations against this man who has worked at the *LA Times*—they came forward. They said certain things. And we can say, you know, we think, well, how should the *LA Times* have handled this, or how should we handle this as a public responding to these allegations?

But what I really don't want to see is saying, well, women have to be quiet. They shouldn't be allowed to talk about what happened between them and men or their experiences or the way that they felt violated. I think the really, really strong thing about #MeToo is that women finally felt like they could come out and say certain things publicly that they've been holding back for a really long time. And I just wouldn't want to go backwards and not have that happen anymore.

MARTIN: Maybe the question becomes down to this whole argument of believe women. What does that mean in this context? Does it mean that women are never to be questioned? Like, what standard of due process and factual investigation apply?

NORTH: I think the most appropriate way to understand that phrase is not that you believe everyone without question but really that you listen. I think what's not OK is to say women shouldn't be talking about this.

MARTIN: Caitlin?

How Will the Topic of Sexual Consent Continue to Evolve?

FLANAGAN: Well, you know, I've had a lot of conversations and with colleagues that are—whom I respect very much at the *Atlantic* about this phrase, believe all women. And I said, I really don't understand it. You know, are we people who just don't lie ever about a sexual encounter? And my colleague explained, just as Anna is, that it's more about listening to women, which I completely understand. But I think language matters, and it's a terribly imprecise term. People who use the phrase—I think they should perhaps change to what Anna's saying in terms of listen to all women.

MARTIN: I just want to be really clear—we're not talking about friends talking to friends or friends talking to private individuals. You're talking about people who are bringing these encounters into the public sphere and demanding a public response. This is the gray area we're talking about here. Anna?

NORTH: I think it makes sense for us to be serious in the way that we interrogate these things. And, of course, we would say, you know, you can't bring a false complaint. But what I don't want to do is say women shouldn't be speaking publicly if what they say is true. Instead, I think we can look at how we're responding.

Something I've been doing a lot of reporting on recently is restorative justice. You know, it doesn't speak necessarily to punish but is about, how do we repair the harm that was done? And I think this is something that has a lot of promise—you know, getting people together, saying, OK. This person feels that they were harmed. What was the harm? How do we make it better? And that's, you know, not necessarily always about someone losing their job. It could be something completely different.

So I think there is really an opportunity for all of us to come together and figure out, you know, how to not have this always be about punishment. In some cases, I think there can be a restorative solution.

MARTIN: I still feel like we're talking past each other here because we're not talking about things that—I mean, the Jonathan Kaiman case is not something that took place in an office. These are two adults of equal stature. He had no control over these women's careers. We're talking about private encounters between two consenting adults where they have very different views about what happened. Caitlin, you have any final thoughts?

FLANAGAN: You want to know what I really think about that?

MARTIN: Yes, I do.

FLANAGAN: Listen—when you're in a private sexual encounter outside of work, and you're in this world that a lot of women fought hard to make where you can have private sexual encounters with men and not be shamed, and when the real problem really comes down to you both had too much to drink or he wasn't very nice to you afterwards. He didn't follow up. He didn't call you. You perceived something later. That is an unfortunate and emotionally painful thing that is part of having a free sexual life, and it usually hits women more hard than it hits men. But that should have no place and no role in any kind of public sphere.

And to turn around your pain, your hurt, your hurt feelings about it and to claim that you are now a victim of some kind of abuse—I think that's a grift because you're stealing from women who fought so hard to tell the truth about sexual assault, and there's long-range consequences. And in the heat of a movement, no one wants to think about long-range consequences. You know, we don't really have any impartial reporters on this because all of us who are women, at some time or another, something bad probably happened to us. So we've all had an experience, and it's there. It can be very hard to keep those experiences out of how we perceive the story or listen to the story.

But I think that a lot of good has been done by the movement, and a lot of damage has been done by the movement. The good outweighs the damage so far. But I don't want to see even in the much smaller sphere the idea that women can have free, consensual sexual relationships with men without strings, and that their hurt feelings can somehow be transubstantiated into an assault story. I think that's ugly.

MARTIN: That was Caitlin Flanagan, contributing editor at *The Atlantic*, and Anna North, senior reporter with *Vox*.
Thank you both so much for talking to us.

FLANAGAN: Thank you.

NORTH: Thank you.

VIEWPOINT 2

> "Many of the young women and girls in my samples not only define sexual consent and sexual assault, but also frame these concepts within the larger cultural, legal and political contexts in which they exist."

Young People Are Using the Internet to Promote Sexual Consent and Education

Chloe Krystyna Garcia

In this viewpoint Chloe Krystyna Garcia discusses how young girls and women are filling in the gaps of formal sex education by creating YouTube videos that address issues like sexual consent and sexual violence, creating a culture in which these topics can be more openly discussed. While sex education in schools is a politicized and controversial topic, leading to discomfort among teachers about teaching certain topics, young YouTubers are able to take a nuanced approach to these topics, going beyond a simple "no means no" and "yes means yes" approach to consent. Girls and young women are also more likely to seek out these videos because they combine sex education with entertainment. Chloe Krystyna Garcia is an instructor on integrated studies in education at McGill University in Montreal, Canada.

"Young People Are Taking Sex-Ed Into Their Own Hands on YouTube," by Chloe Krystyna Garcia, The Conversation, March 2, 2020, https://theconversation.com/young-people-are-taking-sex-ed-into-their-own-hands-on-youtube-131666. Licensed under CC BY-ND 4.0 International.

How Will the Topic of Sexual Consent Continue to Evolve?

As you read, consider the following questions:

1. According to Garcia, why is it important that young female YouTubers explore sexual consent and assault within the context of larger social, legal, and political issues?
2. What techniques do female YouTubers use to make their sex education videos engaging?
3. What are some of the potentially harmful aspects of getting sex education resources from YouTube?

Sex education in Canadian schools continues to be highly politicized and young people are paying the price.

In Québec, for example, the provincial sexual health curriculum has shifted a few times in the last couple of decades, often leaving teachers and schools confused about the approach and the implementation guidelines. In Ontario, sexual health curriculum is also at the mercy of the province's political climate.

In many Canadian classrooms, factors like inadequate teacher training and discomfort impact what topics are addressed or avoided. Unfortunately, these circumstances mean that youth may not get the information they need to engage in healthy, positive sexual relationships.

Meanwhile, sexual health resources flourish online. Studies show that many youth seek out information about sexuality in digital spaces. Within today's participatory social media platforms and networks, many of these resources are produced by youth, for youth. Young girls and women specifically are taking sex education into their own hands.

As a doctoral student at McGill University and a sex education practitioner, I have had the privilege of studying how young YouTubers use their media to talk to their audiences about sexual violence and sexual consent, both in my own dissertation and in collaborative research. In these studies, I looked at a mix of

> ## Teaching Abstinence Only Is Not the Answer
>
> Two scientific review papers find abstinence-only-until-marriage programs and policies in the United States are ineffective because they do not delay sexual initiation or reduce sexual risk behaviors. According to the researchers, these programs also violate adolescent human rights, withhold medically accurate information, stigmatize or exclude many youth, reinforce harmful gender stereotypes, and undermine public health programs.
>
> "The weight of scientific evidence shows these programs do not help young people delay initiation of sexual intercourse," says co-author John Santelli, professor of Population and Family Health at the Mailman School. "While abstinence is theoretically effective, in actual practice, intentions to abstain from sexual activity often fail. These programs simply do not prepare young people to avoid unwanted pregnancies or sexually transmitted diseases."
>
> Abstinence-only-until-marriage approaches have set back sex education, family planning, and HIV-prevention efforts. Between 2002 and 2014, the percentage of schools in the U.S. that require students to learn about human sexuality fell from 67 percent to 48 percent, and requirements for HIV prevention declined from 64 percent to 41 percent. In 1995, 81 percent of adolescent males

YouTube videos and vlogs (or video logs) from youth of all genders, aged between 14 and 30 years old.

Female YouTubers as Sex Educators

The YouTubers in my study, including celebrity vloggers like Meghan Hughes, Laci Green and Hannah Witton, tackle many facets of sexual consent and sexual violence in their videos. They move beyond the oversimplified "no means no" and "yes means yes" messaging that permeates consent education.

Many of the young women and girls in my samples not only define sexual consent and sexual assault, but also frame these

How Will the Topic of Sexual Consent Continue to Evolve?

> and 87 percent of adolescent females reported receiving formal instruction about birth control methods; by 2011-2013, only 55 percent of young men and 60 percent of young women said the same.
>
> By contrast, comprehensive sex education programs, have favorable effects on adolescent behaviors, including sexual initiation, number of sex partners, frequency of sexual activity, use of condoms and contraception, frequency of unprotected sexual activity, STIs, and pregnancy. "Young people have a right to sex education that gives them the information and skills they need to stay safe and healthy," says Leslie Kantor, assistant professor of Population and Family Health at the Mailman School of Public Health and vice president of Education at Planned Parenthood Federation of America. "Withholding critical health information from young people is a violation of their rights. Abstinence-only-until-marriage programs leave all young people unprepared and are particularly harmful to young people who are sexually active, who are LGBTQ, or have experienced sexual abuse."
>
> "Adolescent sexual and reproductive health promotion should be based on scientific evidence and understanding, public health principles, and human rights," says Santelli. "Abstinence-only-until-marriage as a basis for health policy and programs should be abandoned."
>
> "Abstinence-Only Education Is a Failure," Columbia University, August 22, 2017.

concepts within the larger cultural, legal and political contexts in which they exist.

This is important; examining sexual violence from these broad lenses helps spotlight rape myths and victim blaming. Helping youth recognize the impacts of sexual violence and the underlining societal beliefs and structures that sustain it is a positive step towards fostering a consent culture.

I found that young women and girls are taking to YouTube for many reasons, notably, to express themselves, to educate, respond to others, share their narratives and promote social change. Within their videos, several of the YouTubers in my studies actively encourage their audiences to respect sexual consent, to support survivors and to fight rape culture—for example, by how they vote.

Similar to young feminist activists in other online spaces, these YouTubers are positioning themselves as agents of change and using their vast networks to make a difference (some have hundreds of thousands of subscribers). Audiences listening to YouTube videos can therefore learn how about the skills and knowledge they need to engage in healthy relationships, and more broadly, to help prevent sexual violence.

I found that these girls and young women address sexual consent and sexual violence in creative and engaging ways. In their videos, they use emotional narratives, snappy media effects, music, examples that resonate with youth realities and informal language.

Their production choices lend to an authentic and conversational feel. In many ways, these videos offer a form of sex edutainment, combining educational elements with entertainment, to attract young YouTube audiences.

YouTube Pitfalls

There are several benefits to learning about sexuality on YouTube: there is a large selection of videos, audiences can watch them 24/7 and there are opportunities for dialogue. However, accessible features also open doors to potential harmful rhetoric.

I found that some YouTubers (male and female) perpetuate harmful stereotypes and misinformation about survivors and sexual violence. Trolls often showed up in the comments. In fairy tales, trolls lurk under bridges waiting for victims they can eat—in the digital spaces I studied, many hid under the cape of free speech and openly mocked female YouTubers, women in general and feminists.

This was not a surprise; it's well known that the internet can be a dangerous space for women and girls. Sarah Banet-Weiser, professor of media and communications at the London School of Economics, correctly describes popular feminism and misogyny as warring ideologies, with digital spaces being one of their battlegrounds. YouTube is no exception.

How Will the Topic of Sexual Consent Continue to Evolve?

Viewers should also be aware of the corporate nature of YouTube. As researcher and lecturer Sophie Bishop points out in her study of beauty vloggers, YouTube's "algorithmic political economy" means the platform will prioritize videos deemed more commercially viable. Some celebrity YouTubers are financially supported by companies, while others are looking for sponsorship—both of which may affect video content and performance. The algorithms also mean a diversity of voices may be left out.

Supporting Youth

Parents can help youth navigate the messages they see on YouTube and elsewhere. You and your child can also play an important role in sexual violence prevention and the promotion of consent culture in the following ways:

- **Ask and listen.** Show interest in what youth are watching, without judgment. Taking the time to listen to them describe the spaces that they occupy can help build the trust needed to talk to them about the messages they consume.
- **Practice critical media literacy skills with your kids.** We cannot control what is said on the internet; however, we can teach youth to be critical of media messages and to be responsible content producers. MediaSmarts has tip sheets for parents.
- **Address the trolls.** Youth already know about trolls. However, it may be helpful to discuss with them how to deal with hateful online comments. There is no best solution: learning more about it may be a good first start.
- **Be prepared for conversations about sexuality and sexual violence.** If you are comfortable talking about consent, have open, non-judgmental conversations. If you aren't comfortable talking about sexuality or consent, or you are aware that your views may not be healthy, help your child find resources (such as GoAskAlice or Amaze) and someone they trust that they can talk to (a family member, or friend or a local community organization).

- **Teach yourself and be prepared to "unlearn."** Rape myths, victim blaming and other harmful views of survivors are perpetuated across all types of media and platforms. Learn about them and reflect on the ways that you can cultivate positive values and beliefs that support healthy relationships and consent culture.

Keep an open mind: this may require questioning your own attitudes, assumptions and behaviors. Your conversations may lead into the social and cultural realities youth are navigating every day.

VIEWPOINT 3

> "Over the past two decades, the Roman Catholic Church in the US—with the archdiocese of Boston in particular—has been embroiled in a series of child sex scandals."

Catholic Church Sex Abuse Must Be Punished and Stopped

BBC

In the following viewpoint the BBC reports on the various Catholic Church sex scandals around the world. By holding clergy and leaders of the Catholic Church accountable, law enforcement indicates that those in power will no longer be able to use their authority with impunity to force victims to engage in sexual activity. However, this culture of accountability is still relatively new, as the viewpoint indicates that many of these crimes were concealed in the past. Furthermore, the Church is not always cooperative in these attempts to address allegations of sexual abuse. While progress has been made to address this global issue, much still must be done to prevent more abuse. The BBC is a British public service broadcaster.

As you read, consider the following questions:

1. Did Belgian clergy cover up the sex scandal that occurred in that country, as reported in the viewpoint?

"Catholic Church sex abuse scandals around the world", BBC, September 14, 2010. Reprinted with permission.

2. How many priests in the U.S. had faced charges related to sex crimes at the time the viewpoint was published, according to the BBC?
3. According to this viewpoint how many people were abused in Switzerland?

Belgium

The bishop of Bruges, Roger Vangheluwe, resigned in April 2010 after admitting that he had sexually abused a boy for years when he was a priest and after being made a bishop.

The scandal drew in the former head of the Catholic Church in Belgium, Cardinal Godfried Danneels, who had advised the victim in April not to go public with his story until Vangheluwe had retired in 2011.

After the Vangheluwe case came to light, a commission set up to investigate the extent of abuse in the Belgian Church received a flood of calls.

Police controversially raided the commission and Church offices, suspecting some evidence was being covered up—but this move was ruled illegal by a Belgian court.

In September 2010 the head of the commission released harrowing details of some 300 cases of alleged sexual abuse by Belgian clergy.

The abuse was found in nearly every diocese, and 13 alleged victims had committed suicide, he said.

However, he found no indication that the Church had systematically sought to cover up cases.

The Church pledged to set up a victims' support centre in a first attempt to rebuild public trust, and to co-operate more with the police.

Ireland

Two major reports into allegations of pedophilia among Irish clergy last year revealed the shocking extent of abuse, cover-ups and hierarchical failings involving thousands of victims, and stretching back decades.

In one, four Dublin archbishops were found to have effectively turned a blind eye to cases of abuse from 1975 to 2004.

The Dublin archdiocese, it said, operated in a culture of concealment, placing the integrity of its institutions above the welfare of the children in its care.

In the wake of the report, all Irish bishops were summoned to the Vatican to give an account of themselves in person before the Pope.

Four bishops, named in the report, handed in their resignations. The Pope accepted two but told the other two he wanted them to continue.

Six months earlier, another report—the result of a nine-year investigation—documented some six decades of physical, sexual and emotional abuse at residential institutions run by 18 religious orders.

With the Church still reeling from the reports' findings, a fresh scandal erupted in March 2010 when it emerged the head of the Irish Catholic Church, Cardinal Sean Brady, was present at meetings in 1975 where children signed vows of silence over complaints against a pedophile priest, Fr Brendan Smyth.

Cardinal Brady resisted calls to resign but issued an apology for mishandling the matter.

A few days later, on 20 March, Pope Benedict XVI apologized to victims of child sex abuse by Catholic priests in Ireland.

He then accepted the resignation of Bishop John Magee, an aide to three popes before being assigned to Ireland, who was found to have mishandled allegations of clerical sex abuse in his County Cork diocese.

Pope Benedict has now appointed a panel of nine prelates to investigate child abuse in Ireland's Catholic institutions.

United States

Over the past two decades, the Roman Catholic Church in the U.S.—with the archdiocese of Boston in particular—has been embroiled in a series of child sex scandals.

There was public outrage after abuses in the 1990s by two Boston priests, Paul Shanley and John Geoghan, came to light, with suspicions that Church leaders had sought to cover up their crimes by moving them from post to post.

In 2002 the then-Pope John Paul II called an emergency meeting with U.S. cardinals, but allegations continued to emerge.

Despite an apology and pledge to take a tougher line, Archbishop Bernard Law resigned over the scandal at the end of the year.

In September 2003, the Boston archdiocese—the fourth-largest in the U.S.—agreed to pay $85m to settle more than 500 civil suits accusing priests of sexual abuse and church officials of concealment.

A report commissioned by the Church the following year said more than 4,000 U.S. Roman Catholic priests had faced sexual abuse allegations in the last 50 years, in cases involving more than 10,000 children—mostly boys.

A series of huge payouts has been made by U.S. diocese to alleged victims of abuse—the largest being some $660m from the Los Angeles Archdiocese in 2007.

During a tour of the U.S. in 2008, the Pope met privately with victims of abuse by priests and spoke of "the pain and the harm inflicted by the sexual abuse of minors."

In March 2010 documents emerged suggesting that Cardinal Joseph Ratzinger, before he became Pope, failed to respond to letters from U.S. clergy about cases of alleged child sex abuse by a priest in Wisconsin.

Archbishops had complained about Fr Lawrence Murphy in 1996 to a Vatican office led by the future Pope, but apparently received no response.

Fr Murphy, who died in 1998, is suspected of having abused some 200 boys at St John's School for the Deaf in St Francis, Wisconsin, between 1950 and 1974.

One of his alleged victims told the BBC the Pope had known for years about the accusations yet failed to take action.

Germany

Since the start of 2010, at least 300 people have made allegations of sexual or physical abuse by priests across the Pope's home country.

Claims are being investigated in 18 of Germany's 27 Roman Catholic dioceses.

Accusations include the abuse of more than 170 children by priests at Jesuit schools, three Catholic schools in Bavaria, and within the Regensburg Domspatzen school boys' choir that was directed for 30 years by Monsignor Georg Ratzinger, the Pope's brother.

In June, prosecutors said they were investigating the head of Germany's Roman Catholic bishops. Archbishop Robert Zollitsch of Freiburg is suspected of allowing the re-appointment of a priest accused of child abuse in 1987. The archdiocese rejected the charge.

In March, Father Peter Hullermann, who was convicted of molesting boys during his time in the archdiocese of Munich and Freising, was suspended from his duties after breaching a ban on working with children.

Days earlier, the Pope's former diocese said Benedict had unwittingly approved housing for Fr Hullermann when serving as archbishop of Munich; the Vatican denounced what it called "aggressive" efforts to link the Pope to the scandal.

The Regensburg diocese confirmed on 22 March new allegations of child sexual abuse against four priests and two nuns, saying most of the incidents occurred in the 1970s.

Two days later the German government announced it was forming a committee of experts to investigate all the abuse claims.

Italy

In June 2010 a high-profile former priest was charged with sexual abuse.

Pierino Gelmini, 85, is alleged to have abused 12 young people at a drug rehabilitation center he founded.

Meanwhile, a number of deaf men have come forward to say they were abused as children at the Antonio Provolo Institute for the Deaf in the northern city of Verona between the 1950s and the 1980s.

The allegations were first reported in the Italian press in January 2009.

Later last year the Associated Press news agency obtained a written statement from 67 of the school's former pupils naming 24 priests, brothers and lay religious men who they accused of sexual abuse, paedophilia and corporal punishment.

The diocese of Verona said it intended to interview the victims following a request from the Vatican to do so.

Netherlands

In March 2010, Dutch bishops ordered an independent inquiry into more than 200 allegations of sexual abuse of children by priests, in addition to three cases dating from 1950 to 1970.

Allegations first centred on Don Rua monastery school in the eastern Netherlands, with people saying they were abused by Catholic priests in the 1960s and 70s.

This prompted dozens more alleged victims from other institutions to come forward.

Austria

A series of claims of sexual abuse by priests has emerged in the Vorarlberg region.

Some 16 people have reported 27 alleged incidents there, spanning half a century.

Ten children are also alleged to have been abused at a monastery in Mehrerau in the 1970s and early 80s.

Meanwhile five priests at a monastery in Kremsmuenster in Upper Austria have been suspended after complaints of sexual and physical abuse of boys there.

Separately, the head of a Salzburg monastery, Bruno Becker, resigned after confessing to having abused a boy 40 years ago, when he was a monk.

Switzerland

A commission set up by the Swiss Bishops Conference in 2002 has been investigating allegations of abuse involving the Catholic Church there.

A member of the commission, Abbot Martin Werlen, said in a newspaper interview this month that about 60 people have said they were abused by Catholic priests. The alleged incidents are reported to have occurred over the past 15 years.

A priest in the canton of Thurgau was arrested on 19 March on suspicion of sexual abuse of minors, police said.

Malta

Three priests have been accused of sexually abusing 10 orphan children in Malta during the 1980s and 1990s.

Pope Benedict visited the island in April and held an emotional meeting with victims, pledging to bring those responsible to justice and to protect young people in the future.

Spain

Police have launched an investigation into three members of staff at a care home run by a Catholic order.

There have also been formal accusations against a Carmelite monk in eastern Spain and Franciscan brothers in the south.

VIEWPOINT 4

> "Consent is much too low a standard for promoting ethical sex—even if it may be the best available legal standard. And focusing on consent limits our ability to create better approaches to dealing with sexual violence."

Sexual Consent Alone Is Not Enough

Nicole M. Jeffrey

In this viewpoint Nicole M. Jeffrey argues that consent shouldn't be the standard for promoting ethical sex and preventing sexual violence. She asserts that it sets the bar too low and should not be the focus of sex education. She points out that even if someone consents to sex, they may not want it or enjoy it, but instead feel pressured to engage in it. She also believes it is ineffective because most sexual violence is not caused by misunderstandings around consent, and the conversations around consent give perpetrators an opportunity to blame the victim by stating they did not communicate clearly enough. Instead, Jeffrey asserts that sex education should focus on teaching young people how to empathize, communicate, and engage in mutual decision-making. Nicole M. Jeffrey is an adjunct assistant professor and postdoctoral fellow in psychology at the University of Windsor in Ontario, Canada.

"Focusing on Consent Ignores Better Ways of Preventing Sexual Violence," by Nicole M. Jeffrey, The Conversation, May 29, 2023, https://theconversation.com/focusing-on-consent-ignores-better-ways-of-preventing-sexual-violence-205631. Licensed under CC BY-ND 4.0 International.

How Will the Topic of Sexual Consent Continue to Evolve?

As you read, consider the following questions:

1. Why does the author say there's little evidence that education about consent reduces sexual violence?
2. How does consent not disrupt stereotypes that perpetuate sexual violence, according to this viewpoint?
3. What does Jeffrey suggest should be taught instead of consent?

In early May, a New York jury found Donald Trump liable for sexually abusing the writer E. Jean Carroll in 1996. The jury did not find him liable for allegedly raping her.

In the wake of this high-profile case, and the many others of the #MeToo movement, what should we be doing to prevent sexual violence and promote equitable sex? So far, consent is getting too much of the spotlight. Schools, universities and popular media are focusing heavily on consent in their efforts to curb high rates of sexual violence.

Many advocates and educators have recently shifted their messaging from "no means no" to "yes means yes" and "consent is sexy." This messaging promotes voluntary and affirmative agreement. That is, the idea that silence does not mean consent.

Regardless, consent is much too low a standard for promoting ethical sex—even if it *may* be the best available legal standard. And focusing on consent limits our ability to create better approaches to dealing with sexual violence.

It's Time to Stop Focusing on Consent

Sexual violence is the use of verbal pressure or physical violence to engage in any sexual activity with someone who is unwilling or hasn't consented. It is most often committed by men against women and other marginalized groups and is supported by societal stereotypes about gender and sexuality.

As part of my research over the past decade, I have interviewed women who were victimized and men who perpetrated sexual violence. I have also conducted focus groups with men about heterosexual sex and dating. My critique of consent is based on this and other research.

Here are five reasons we should stop focusing on consent and start thinking about more ethical values and norms.

Consensual Sex Is Not Always Wanted, Pleasurable or Free from Coercion

People can consent to sex they don't want or enjoy. Women often agree to sex they don't want to avoid hurting a partner's feelings, to maintain a relationship or to be seen as a good partner.

People can also obtain consent by pressuring or coercing someone. Men are more likely than women to use violence and coercion in order to obtain someone's consent, often after they've gently declined.

Messaging about consent like "no means no" and "yes means yes" implies that it's okay to continue trying if one's partner hasn't clearly said "yes" or "no."

Teaching People How to Give and Understand Consent Isn't Going to Prevent Sexual Violence Because Sexual Violence Isn't Usually About Misunderstanding

There's little to no evidence that education about consent reduces sexual violence. Most men already understand when women don't want to have sex, even without a firm "no." And knowing how to ask for consent isn't going to stop those who choose to ignore refusals or use violence. In the context of men's sexual violence against women, consent doesn't change men's feelings of entitlement to sex and women's bodies.

In the words of one woman I interviewed who was victimized:

He didn't necessarily . . . force himself upon me, but . . . he knew that there wasn't really consent. Like I gave it, but not really fully.

Consent Doesn't Require Meaningful, Collaborative Decision-Making Between Partners

Consent boils down to one partner's agreement in response to another's request. It is insufficient for promoting deeper collaboration in deciding whether and how sex will take place. In the case of sex between women and men, this usually means that men's desires are prioritized. Consent is also something you do *before* sex, rather than an ongoing and embedded *part* of sex.

Consent Doesn't Disrupt the Stereotypes that Support Sexual Violence

For example, false stereotypes suggest men can't control their sex drives. Some men use these stereotypes to claim it's not right or fair for their partners to change their minds or stop sex once started or consented to.

The expectation that sex should be natural and spontaneous can make it difficult for women to stop unwanted sex. It also means that many young people view consent as disruptive to this "natural" progression.

Consent Can Be Used as an Excuse for Sexual Violence

It allows perpetrators to justify sexual violence because they can claim the victim gave unclear responses. Popular consent messages like "yes means yes" and "no means no" are easily co-opted and provide a ready-made excuse.

For example, men in two of my studies used the importance of consent to blame sexual violence on women for not clearly communicating their lack of consent. And because we often see communication as being up to women, these men didn't need to take any responsibility for asking or clarifying.

One perpetrator I interviewed even referred specifically to a consent message heard on campus to simultaneously admit that he should have listened to his partner while blaming her:

> *I also told her to maybe be a bit more direct when it comes to 'Yes' and 'No,' because she was providing answers that were a little*

cloudy. Which I know with all the consent stuff up on the walls here it's, you know, 'only yes means yes.'

If Not Consent, then What?

Moving beyond the language of consent will open new possibilities for promoting truly equitable and ethical sex. At a minimum, we need to teach young people how to communicate more meaningfully about sex.

We need to teach that empathy, mutual decision-making and ongoing communication are integral components of sex, rather than preconditions that only take place before sex. And we need to teach and expect boys and men to listen to women's desires and care about their well-being.

Reducing sexual violence and promoting ethical sex is also going to require substantial cultural change. Prevention programs that, in part, challenge what it means to relate as women and men are some of the most effective at reducing sexual violence. Comprehensive sexual health education that teaches young people about these issues early in life is also essential.

The idea of consent should have never had more than a supporting role in defining ethical sex. It's time to shift the spotlight.

Periodical and Internet Sources Bibliography

The following articles have been selected to supplement the diverse views presented in this chapter.

Grant Hilary Brenner, "Sexual Consent Among Emerging Adults: A Leading Edge of Social Change," Psychology Today, February 16, 2022. https://www.psychologytoday.com/us/blog/experimentations/202202/sexual-consent-among-emerging-adults-leading-edge-social-change.

Billy Cao, "Transcending Sexual Consent," the *Duke Chronicle*, September 9, 2022. https://www.dukechronicle.com/article/2022/09/090922-cao-consent.

Megan Carvajal, "Opinion: Schools Should Prioritize Teaching Youth About Sexual Consent," the *Colorado Sun*, September 12, 2021. https://coloradosun.com/2021/09/12/sex-education-consent-schools-opinion/.

Christine Emba, "Consent is Not Enough. We Need a New Sexual Ethic," the *Washington Post*, March 17, 2022. https://www.washingtonpost.com/opinions/2022/03/17/sex-ethics-rethinking-consent-culture/.

Luba Fein, "Has the Nordic Model Worked? What Does the Research Say?," Nordic Model Now, December 22, 2019. https://nordicmodelnow.org/2019/12/22/has-the-nordic-model-worked-what-does-the-research-say/.

Brett Henebery, "Why Evidence-Led Consent Education is Essential," the *Educator*, May 1, 2023. https://www.theeducatoronline.com/k12/news/why-evidenceled-consent-education-is-essential/282381.

Carlos Jamieson, "State Approaches to Teach Consent in Health Education Classrooms," Education Commission of the United States, April 27, 2022. https://www.ecs.org/state-approaches-to-teach-consent-in-health-education-classrooms/.

Charlotte Rogers, "Consent Education: Why It Matters and How to Promote It in Your Community," Our Wave, June 16, 2023. https://www.ourwave.org/post/consent-education-why-it-matters-and-how-to-promote-it-in-your-community#:~:text=Consent%20education%20ensures%20 no%20one,is%20revisited%20over%20the%20years.

Tife Sanusi, "Why Does Consent Need to be Taught in Schools? We Asked 2 Incredible Activists in Nigeria," Global Citizen, January 25, 2022. https://www.globalcitizen.org/en/content/consent-education-schools-universities-nigeria/.

Essi Thesslund, "The False Promise of the Nordic Model of Sex Work," Open Democracy, April 17, 2018. https://www.opendemocracy.net/en/beyond-trafficking-and-slavery/false-promise-of-nordic-model-of-sex-work/.

For Further Discussion

Chapter 1
1. Based on what you've read in this chapter, how would you define sexual consent? Use evidence from two viewpoints to back up your definition.
2. How common is sexual violence, according to viewpoints in this chapter? Do the statistics surprise you?
3. Why is sexual consent on college campuses such a complicated issue? Use facts from the viewpoints to argue your case.

Chapter 2
1. How does culture support patriarchal attitudes and beliefs, according to viewpoints in this chapter?
2. Does social media have a role in combatting sexual assault? Does it have any negative cultural impacts that can promote sexual violence? Explain your answer using examples from this chapter.
3. How can religious beliefs make it difficult for people to have a say in sexual consent matters? Use evidence from viewpoints in this chapter to support your argument.

Chapter 3
1. Is supporting sex work feminist? Use arguments from viewpoints in this chapter to support your answer.
2. What are some of the impacts of the criminalization of sex work mentioned in this chapter?
3. Should sex work be decriminalized? Support your argument with details from at least two different viewpoints.

Chapter 4

1. Based on what you've read in the viewpoints in this chapter and throughout the book, who should be responsible for sex education? What should they teach?
2. How have those with authority used their position to force sexual activity? Use examples from at least two viewpoints in this chapter.
3. Do you think consent is enough to make sex ethical? Why or why not?

Organizations to Contact

The editors have compiled the following list of organizations concerned with the issues debated in this book. The descriptions are derived from materials provided by the organizations. All have publications or information available for interested readers. The list was compiled on the date of publication of the present volume; the information provided here may change. Be aware that many organizations take several weeks or longer to respond to inquiries, so allow as much time as possible.

American Civil Liberties Union (ACLU)
125 Broad Street, 18th Floor
New York, NY 10004
(212) 549-2500
website: www.aclu.org

The America Civil Liberties Union seeks to create a more equal United States by expanding the reach of the Constitution. They fight for equal rights on many current issues including women's rights, LGBTQ+ rights, disability rights, and many other areas.

Amnesty International
311 W. 43rd Street, 7th Floor
New York, NY 10036
(212) 807-8400
website: www.amnestyusa.org

Amnesty International is an organization that works to guarantee that human rights are enjoyed by all. They are hard at work seeking justice in a variety of modern issues, including gender and sexuality justice.

Center for Constitutional Rights

666 Broadway, 7th Floor
New York, NY 10012
(212) 614-6464
website: https://ccrjustice.org/

The Center for Constitutional Rights fights for liberation and justice for marginalized groups. This organization works for many important issues of today, including preventing sexual and gender-based violence.

The Guttmacher Institute

125 Maiden Lane, 7th Floor
New York, NY 10038
(212) 248-1111
website: www.guttmacher.org

The Guttmacher Institute is a research and policy organization that aims to protect sexual and reproductive rights around the world. The organization maintains an online presence focused on quality research which forms the basis for its informative articles, fact sheets, and work.

Human Rights Watch (HRW)

350 5th Ave., 34th Floor
New York, NY 10118-3299
(212) 290-4700
website: www.hrw.org

Human Rights Watch is a worldwide organization dedicated to protecting the rights of individuals and saving lives. The advocates at HRW work in close to 100 countries around the globe investigating, reporting, and working to end abuse.

Humphrey School of Public Affairs

130 Humphrey School, 301 19th Ave., South
Minneapolis, MN 55455
(612) 626-8910
email: hhhadmit@umn.ed
website: www.hhh.umn.edu/

The Hubert H. Humphrey School of Public Affairs hosts the Center on Women, Gender, and Public Policy. Research done here shines a light on gender-based policies that impact communities throughout the U.S. and around the world.

National Center on Sexual Exploitation

1201 F St., NW, Suite 200
Washington, DC 20004
(202) 393-7245
website: https://endsexualexploitation.org/

The National Center on Sexual Exploitation has a clear mission: They exist to build a world where people can live and love without sexual exploitation or abuse. They are working to end child sexual abuse, prostitution, sex trafficking, and more.

National Organization of Men Against Sexism

3500 E. 17th Avenue
Denver, CO 80206
(303) 997-9581
email: info@nomas.org
website: https://nomas.org/

The National Organization of Men Against Sexism is an organization supporting changes that promote equality and justice in numerous areas. They are pro-feminism, supportive of LGBTQ+ rights, anti-racist, and more.

National Sexual Violence Resource Center
2101 N. Front Street, Governor's Plaza North Building #2
Harrisburg, PA 17110
(877) 739-3895
website: www.nsvrc.org

The National Sexual Violence Resource Center provides research and tools to people working in their communities to end sexual harassment, assault, and abuse. This center has a large database of information about sexual consent issues.

Open Society Foundations
224 W. 57th Street
New York, NY 10019
(212) 548-0600
website: www.opensocietyfoundations.org

The Open Society Foundation is a privately funded organization that supports various groups working for justice, democratic ideals, and human rights. Some groups supported by the society work on sexual justice areas.

Bibliography of Books

Leah Aguirre. *The Girl's Guide to Relationships, Sexuality, & Consent: Tools to Help Teens Stay Safe, Empowered, & Confident.* Oakland, CA: Instant Help Books, 2022.

Hailey Bondy. *#MeToo and You: Everything You Need to Know About Consent, Boundaries, and More.* Minneapolis, MN: Zest Books, 2021.

Cheryl M. Bradshaw. *Real Talk About Sex & Consent: What Every Teen Needs to Know.* Oakland, CA: Instant Help Books, 2020.

Donna Freitas. *The Big Questions Book of Sex and Consent.* New York, NY: Levine Querido, 2020.

Leigh Gilmore. *The #MeToo Effect: What Happens When We Believe Women.* New York, NY: Columbia University Press, 2023.

Heather Hudak. *#MeToo Movement.* New York, NY: Crabtree Publishing Company, 2019.

Monica Mehta. *It's Totally Normal: An LGBTQIA+ Guide to Puberty, Sex, and Gender.* London, UK: Jessica Kingsley Publishers, 2023.

Peggy Parks. *The #MeToo Movement.* San Diego, CA: Reference Point Press, 2020.

Ace Ratcliff. *Disabilities, Sexual Health, and Consent.* New York, NY: Rosen YA, 2020.

Naomi Rockler. *Understanding Consent and Boundaries: Dating and Relationships in the #MeToo Era.* San Diego, CA: Reference Point Press, 2024.

Yumi Stynes. *Welcome to Consent: How to Say No, When to Say Yes, and How to Be the Boss of Your Body.* Somerville, MA, 2023.

Pete Wallis. *What Does Consent Really Mean?* Philadelphia, PA: Jessica Kingsley Publishers, 2018.

Index

A

abstinence, 16, 148–149
affirmative consent, 25–30, 43–44
age of consent, 14, 28–29, 33
alcohol/drugs, 18, 22–23, 28, 31–34, 68, 81, 99
Aldridge, Alex, 31–34
American Civil Liberties Union, 92
American Sexual Health Association, 14
Amnesty International, 129–133
A-21, 94

B

Bateman, Victoria, 107–122
Biden, Joe, 15, 40
body language, 22
Burgin, Rachael, 25–30
Bush, George W., 96–97

C

Caine, Christine, 94–96, 98–99
Carter, Jimmy, 130
Centers for Disease Control and Prevention, 38
Coalition Against Trafficking in Women, 131
college, 18, 35–48, 67, 72, 77, 99, 161

Concerned Women for America, 95
Cook, Joan M., 79–83
Coo, Sarah L., 35–41

D

Daniel-Hughes, Carly, 93–100
disability, 33, 103, 105, 112

E

Ellis, Amy, 79–83

F

feminism, 93–100, 108, 110–113, 115–117, 120–121, 150
Flanagan, Caitlin, 137–145
Force: Upsetting the Culture of Rape, 47
4 Every Girl, 62

G

Garcia, Chloe Krystyna, 146–152
Grant, Melissa Gira, 95–96
Grimley, Naomi, 129–133

H

health,
 mental, 58, 60, 62, 79–83, 99, 103
 physical, 58, 80–81, 124

Index

reproductive, 21, 33, 45, 95, 148–149
sexual, 21, 33, 81, 92, 128, 147–149
Hendriks, Jacqueline, 19–24
homelessness, 99
human trafficking, 93–100, 125–127, 129, 131

I

immigration, 99, 125–126, 128
implied consent, 27–28, 30
internet, 101–106, 125, 127–128, 146–152

J

Jeffrey, Nicole M., 160–164
Jensen, Robert, 64–72
Jones, Angela, 101–106
justice system, 15, 26–29, 34, 44–48, 54, 65, 68–71, 95, 99, 102, 108, 115, 125–127, 130, 154

K

Keller, Jessalynn, 73–78

L

laws, 14–15, 25–30, 46–47, 55, 92–100, 105–106, 114, 118, 120, 123–133
LGBTQIA+, 33, 38, 51, 79–83, 95, 98, 103–104, 124–126, 128, 162
Lowik, Vicki, 84–88

M

Martin, Michel, 138–145
media/popular culture, 15, 40, 51–52, 58–63, 66
MeToo movement, 51, 73–78, 137–145, 161
military, 38–39, 83

N

Nagle, Rebecca, 47–48
National Center for Transgender Equality, 92
North, Anna, 137–145

O

Obama, Barack, 44
objectification of women, 58–63, 66, 70–71, 121

P

patriarchy, 15, 31–33, 51–52, 59, 61, 64–72, 108–109, 112
Perkins, Djuna, 46–47
personal boundaries, 22–23
pink tax, 59–60
Planned Parenthood, 14, 149
pornography, 32, 66, 70, 72, 102, 104–105, 117, 119
power dynamics, 20, 23, 31–33, 66–67, 70–72, 84–88

R

race, 33, 38, 108, 111, 124, 127–128

Rape, Abuse and Incest National Network, 65, 71
Raphael, Jody, 70–71
religion, 15, 51–52, 82, 84–88, 92–100, 109–110, 119, 137, 153–159

S

Sen, Swagata, 58–63
sex education, 15–16, 18–30, 39, 55, 137, 146–152, 160–162, 164
sexual violence, 14–15, 18, 20, 23, 26, 29–30, 32–41, 45, 51, 53–58, 61, 64–88, 92–93, 95, 105, 108–109, 115, 117–120, 123–128, 130, 146–164
sexual/body terminology, 22
sex work, 15, 32, 70, 92–133
Sherman, Yvonne, 97
Smith, Tovia, 42–48
social/economic class, 33, 38, 56, 99, 102, 108
social media, 51, 73–78, 147
Spellman, Mary, 43–44
Spurill, Marjorie, 95
Swift, Jayne, 123–128

T

Taylor, Annabel, 84–88
Trump, Donald, 36, 40–41, 97, 161

U

UNICEF, 51

V

victim blaming, 28–29, 40, 53–57, 65, 70, 80–81, 149, 152, 160, 163–164

W

Warshaw, Robin, 37
Watson-Lynn, Erin, 53–57
Weinstein, Harvey, 74, 77
Wellspring Living, 95
withdrawn consent, 14–15, 22, 43, 163
Women Against Pornography, 117
Women's Christian Temperance Union, 14
World Charter for Prostitutes' Rights, 111